Management
Matters

PEARSON

At Pearson, we believe in learning – all kinds of learning for all kinds of people. Whether it's at home, in the classroom or in the workplace, learning is the key to improving our life chances.

That's why we're working with leading authors to bring you the latest thinking and the best practices, so you can get better at the things that are important to you. You can learn on the page or on the move, and with content that's always crafted to help you understand quickly and apply what you've learned.

If you want to upgrade your personal skills or accelerate your career, become a more effective leader or more powerful communicator, discover new opportunities or simply find more inspiration, we can help you make progress in your work and life.

Pearson is the world's leading learning company. Our portfolio includes the Financial Times, Penguin, Dorling Kindersley, and our educational business, Pearson International.

Every day our work helps learning flourish, and wherever learning flourishes, so do people.

To learn more please visit us at: **www.pearson.com/uk**

Management
Matters

From the humdrum to the big decisions

Philip Delves Broughton

PEARSON

Harlow, England • London • New York • Boston • San Francisco • Toronto • Sydney
Auckland • Singapore • Hong Kong • Tokyo • Seoul • Taipei • New Delhi
Cape Town • São Paulo • Mexico City • Madrid • Amsterdam • Munich • Paris • Milan

PEARSON EDUCATION LIMITED
Edinburgh Gate
Harlow CM20 2JE
United Kingdom
Tel: +44 (0)1279 623623
Fax: +44 (0)1279 431059
Website: www.pearson.com/uk

First published in Great Britain in 2012 (print and electronic)

© Philip Delves Broughton 2012 (print and electronic)

The right of Philip Delves Broughton to be identified as author of this work has been asserted by him in accordance with the Copyright, Designs and Patents Act 1988.

Pearson Education is not responsible for the content of third-party internet sites.

ISBN: 978-0-273-78135-6 (print)
ISBN: 978-0-273-78864-5 (epub)
ISBN: 978-0-273-78865-2 (PDF)

British Library Cataloguing-in-Publication Data
A catalogue record for this book is available from the British Library

Library of Congress Cataloging-in-Publication Data
A catalog record for this book is available from the Library of Congress

The Financial Times. With a worldwide network of highly respected journalists, *The Financial Times* provides global business news, insightful opinion and expert analysis of business, finance and politics. With over 500 journalists reporting from 50 countries worldwide, our in-depth coverage of international news is objectively reported and analysed from an independent global perspective. To find out more, visit www.ft.com/pearsonoffer

10 9 8 7 6 5 4 3 2 1
16 15 14 13 12

Typeset in 10pt Plantin by 30
Printed and bound in Great Britain by Ashford Colour Press Ltd, Gosport

NOTE THAT ANY PAGE CROSS REFERENCES REFER TO THE PRINT EDITION

Contents

Acknowledgements

Many thanks to my professors at Harvard Business School for introducing me to many of the ideas in this book; to Joel Podolny at Apple, to Carl Schramm, Bo Fishback, Dane Stangler and Nick Seguin, all at various times at the Kauffman Foundation for Entrepreneurship and Education, for many conversations on this vast subject, and also to Luke Bridgeman and James Lyle. To Alec Russell, Ravi Mattu, Harriet Arnold, Emma Jacobs and Gautam Malkani at *The Financial Times* for their interest, editing and ideas. To Liz Gooster for getting this project off the ground, to Richard Pigden for his help with permissions, and Nicole Eggleton and Melanie Carter for getting it all finished. And, as ever, to my family.

Publisher's acknowledgements

We are grateful to Larry Hirschhorn for permission to reproduce the figure on p. 62, which is taken from Hirschhorn, Larry, *Managing in the New Team Environment: Skills, Tools, and Methods*. San Jose, CA: Authors Choice Press, © 2002. Reprinted with permission.

All material taken from *The Financial Times* reprinted with permission © The Financial Times Limited. Full copies of all the articles used in this work can be found in the appendix at the back of the book.

In some instances we have been unable to trace the owners of copyright material, and we would appreciate any information that would enable us to do so.

About the author

Philip Delves Broughton was born in Bangladesh, raised and educated in the United Kingdom, obtained his BA at Oxford University, and now lives in the United States. He reported from over 25 countries as a foreign correspondent for *The Daily Telegraph* of London before getting his MBA at Harvard Business School. He has since worked as a writer at Apple Inc. and the Kauffman Foundation for Entrepreneurship and Education, and as a contributing columnist at the *Financial Times*. His writing has appeared in *The Wall Street Journal* and *The Atlantic*. He is the author of *What They Teach You at Harvard Business School: My Two Years Inside the Cauldron of Capitalism* (2008), a *New York Times* bestseller and a *Financial Times* and *USA Today* business book of the year, and *Life's A Pitch: What the World's Best Sales People Can Teach Us All* (2012).

Introduction: What is management?

In 1999, soon after the sex scandal which very nearly sunk his Presidency, Bill Clinton turned to NASA with a very curious request. The 30th anniversary of the moon landings were coming up and he wanted a piece of moon rock, a 3.6 billion year old lump, to sit on a table in the Oval Office. Meetings in the White House at the time were fractious. Everyone was angry with Clinton for what he had done. The mood in Washington was tense and more argumentative than usual. The rock served as a reality check. As Clinton later explained: 'When people started the crazy stuff, I'd say, "Wait a minute, guys. See that rock, it's 3.6 billion years old. We're all just passing through, take a break, calm down, let's see what makes sense." It had an incredible calming effect!' Clinton's moon rock was an example of managerial genius.

In 2011, Sir Alex Ferguson, the manager of Manchester United Football Club celebrated 25 years in the job. In a business where two years is considered equivalent to tenure, Ferguson's longevity and success attracts profound admiration. The newspapers in Britain were filled with eulogies to Ferguson. Photo spreads were arranged to show us what the Britain of 1986 looked like, who ran the country and who topped the charts. Former opponents testified to his tactical genius during matches, while ex-players spoke of his managerial gifts, his ability to burrow inside the heads of every individual and find the right buttons to press in order to extract their very best performance.

Observers of the game credited his success to his 'hunger', a need to succeed instilled when he was a boy growing up in one of the roughest parts of Glasgow. Even with all his success and his championships, he still cannot sleep after a loss, churning over his mistakes, but resolving at dawn to find the best in every defeat. Ferguson himself said that he has been able to adapt to meet the changing demands of his sport, the impact of globalisation, of salaries spiralling upwards, of innovations in sports science. Management, he said, is not a static skill.

Yet on the other hand, a rival manager, Kenny Dalglish of Liverpool, said that Ferguson's success came down to the fact that 'he has always been the same'. His virtues and principles have remained unchanged. He has changed what needed to be changed while leaving the fundamentals well alone.

These habits also proved contagious. 'He breathes the club', one of his ex-players said of him. 'He comes in every morning, he's in before every single player, every single staff member. He's hungry. And it rubs off on everyone.' But not all of those habits were pleasant. As one former player, Steve Bruce, said, in order to motivate his players Ferguson would administer a technique known as the 'hairdryer treatment'. He would 'just shout right in your face. We all answered him back, but there was only ever one winner – him, and rightly so. It made you better and it made you stronger.' And once it was over, Ferguson never held it against you. He would simply expect you to do better next time.

Management is full of such contradictions. Some managers thrive by setting a terrific example, while never raising their voice. Others succeed by creating a state of constant tension and unease.

Ricky Gervais, the creator of *The Office*, says the key to management is 'to be up-front and fair. Then, people might not like what you do because they're getting the thick end of the wedge, but they can't have you on it.'[1] Steve Jobs, the venerated founder and chief

---

[1] Interview, *Harvard Business Review*, April 2011, p. 140

executive of Apple, thought nothing of humiliating and abusing people if he thought it would push them to better work. There are managers who like to be liked, and those who would rather be admired or even feared. There are those who like to do everything and others who succeed by delegating.

Whenever Jobs promoted an employee to the rank of Vice President at Apple, he would tell them what he expected of them by comparing their work to that of the janitor. If the rubbish in his office was not being emptied regularly, for whatever reason, he would ask the janitor why. The janitor could easily offer an excuse. The lock on the door was changed, perhaps, and he couldn't get hold of a key. From a janitor, such an excuse was acceptable. He did not have the tools at his disposal to get the key. 'When you're the janitor, reasons matter', Jobs would tell the new Vice President. But 'somewhere between the janitor and the CEO, reasons stop mattering'. Jobs believed the Rubicon is 'crossed when you become a VP'. In other words you no longer have any excuses for failing. You are now responsible. If what you have been asked to and agreed to do does not happen, you are entirely responsible, no matter what has got in your way.[2]

Managers may live on either side of Jobs's organisational Rubicon. Some will have the authority and resources they need to do what they do. Others will have a more limited set of powers and responsibilities. But if they hope to succeed, both groups will have to prove, like the Apple VP, that they can be effective. That when given a problem to solve, they are the best person available to get it solved. The great Japanese industrialist Eiichi Shibusawa used to say that the essence of the manager was not rank or money, but responsibility.

> the essence of the manager: not rank or skill but responsibility

---

[2] 'How Apple Works: Inside the World's Biggest Start-up', Adam Lashinsky, *Fortune Magazine*, 23 May 2011

This is at the core of what we mean by management. Techniques will change, as will roles. Today you may be asked to be an 'integrator' of many business functions, and tomorrow asked to focus narrowly on one. One project may require that you manage a multinational team across several time zones, meeting them only via videoconference to meet a looming deadline. Another will require that you find five people down the corridor, put them in a single room and set up a two-year plan. One crisis might require restoring a large existing business to health, another might demand you start a new business from scratch.

The leader of an organisation can be expected to set strategy, to deliver speeches and pull people along at a high level. But it is the responsibility of the manager, buried at various levels in an organisation, to turn ideas and words into action and output, whether product or financial returns on invested capital.

> it's the manager's responsibility to turn ideas and words into action and output

In short, a lot is asked of managers, even as we question their very right to exist. Scare-mongering about the demise of the middle manager – like the collapse of the housing market or the rising cost of sending one's progeny to university – is guaranteed to send the stress levels of the professional middle class into overdrive. New technology is said to have managers in its sights. There are those who say the era of the manager is over, that the gap between senior executives and the ground floor operations of a business can now be filled by software, by monitoring systems which can create reports and presentations, and by low-cost administrative support found in faraway countries. Managers are derided as shallow generalists, 20th century beings whose time has passed. The future belongs to creators and innovators, not the dinosaurs who once kept everything moving.

There is evidence to support this view. Senior executives in recent years have taken advantage of the rise in financial leverage to reward themselves with ever larger compensation plans, while middle managers have seen their salaries stagnate. Once upon a time, middle management was perceived as a promising career path to the top, but no longer. Nowadays, even after years of experience as a middle manager, it is not uncommon to see the top jobs snapped up by former consultants or by young MBAs.

But there is something obnoxious about the dehumanising idea that companies will soon be made up of self-managing creative teams and executives, with nothing in between. In fact, this argument rests on an outmoded idea of the manager, articulated by the great business historian Alfred Chandler in his 1977 book *The Visible Hand*. In his classic analysis of the rise of American corporations from the 19th to the 20th century, Chandler attributed a central coordinating role to middle managers of, on the one hand, conveying information to and from the executives and workers on the production line, and on the other, of driving functional efficiencies in the system designed by executives, which led to, for instance, better managed sales forces, lower pricing and improved channels of distribution.

Technology has created systems which are undoubtedly more efficient and cheaper than humans at serving these functions. But, like any living organism, companies have responded by developing different needs. Corporations today are more complex and adaptive than the vast, hierarchical structures Chandler described. And in this structure, managers are expected to do more, not less. For all of technology's power, there are many things it cannot yet do. It cannot give chief executives a clear view of their operations from top to bottom. It cannot tell you if a star salesman is unhappy or a competitor is about to launch a rival product. It cannot deal with harassment claims or set a tactical objective.

The global financial crisis which began in 2008 revealed how little executives knew about what was going on inside their organisations. An excessive faith in financial models and computerised risk systems led them to miss what a responsible manager could have told them: that at the retail level, they were making too many loans to people who could never pay them back, and mis-pricing their risk.

Companies and their leaders still depend on managers to tell them what is going on and to manage the endless unanticipated crises which occur in an organisation. Managers today are expected to be agile problem solvers, capable of managing dynamic situations and solving problems wherever and whenever they occur. The challenges of management are always changing, but they remain as relevant as ever.

Steven Spear, a senior lecturer at MIT and author of *The High-Velocity Edge*, offers two persuasive analogies between businesses and armies and the human body. For all the sophistication of modern warfare, armies still need non-commissioned officers and officers to provide the link between generals and privates. By analogy, one could say that the human body has its own strata of middle management which coordinate the work of cells, tissues and organs with the brain. Direct communication between the cells and the brain minus the intermediary layers woud mean not just a different structure for coordination but a less efficient one.

Fred Hassan, the chairman of Bausch & Lomb and a seasoned pharmaceutical executive, has written that 'the managers most responsible for a company's success or failure happen to be the ones with whom the CEO spends the least amount of time. The people I'm talking about are frontline managers – shop-floor supervisors, leaders of R&D or sales teams, managers in restaurant chains or call centers.' He made the point that it is these frontline managers who 'must motivate and bolster the morale of the people who do the work – those who design, make and sell the products or deliver service to customers'.[3]

It may be the CEOs who hog the limelight, but it is the managers who execute a company's strategy. Hassan recommended that CEOs do more than simply manage by walking around. He suggested they

---

[3] 'The Frontline Advantage', Fred Hassan, *Harvard Business Review*, May 2011

get right down in the trenches alongside the managers, to make sure they are doing their best work. As companies change more quickly than at any time in history, the lower CEOs must work in their organisation. They must seek out those managers capable of becoming 'passionate drivers', people inside the company capable of challenging old methods and puzzling out the new. Even the best strategic plans will founder if the managers charged with implementing them are not motivated or given the resources to do so.

> it is the managers who execute a company's strategy

Hassan suggested that CEOs should convene groups of frontline managers in every area of their operations and make sure to talk to them as frequently as they would customers or the strategic planning team. While he was CEO of Schering-Plough, the issues which bubbled up to Hassan during these meetings seemed trivial at first. A team of salesmen in Russia complained about the lengthy procedure for getting a car for a new rep. A tedious, bureaucratic issue, surely. But the harder he looked, Hassan found a deeper problem. Great salesmen didn't want to take the bus to see customers. They would simply find an employer who gave them a car immediately. The car was not the issue. It was the fact that his company was losing high-performing salesmen to rivals. The frustration with the car procedure was indicative of a broader bureaucratic problem. Too much paperwork, too many rules were constraining his company's growth. This one simple issue triggered an overhaul of Schering-Plough's Russian operations to make them more flexible and entrepreneurial, and led to rapid growth.

No technology could have alerted Hassan to the problem with the salesmen's cars.

Ultimately, managers will survive because of what their critics see as their greatest weakness: their humanity. Business is changing more quickly now than ever before, scampering desperately after advances in technology. Human beings remain the most adaptable management tools any executive could want. They can learn, lead, change, haggle, calculate, persuade, emote and inspire.

The need for managers will not bite the dust because managers give a great company its heart beat.

Managers require a range of talents. At various times they must be specialists and generalists, learners and teachers, collaborators and sole performers, leaders and followers. It is up to managers then to keep learning and making themselves useful. In a previous era, I might have called the first chapter 'Managing your career'. But that would suggest you have more control than in fact you do. What you can manage is yourself, in the hope that a rewarding career ensues.

One of the major trends any manager must take account of is the flattening of organisations. Hierarchies are less common and more is expected of a manager than ever. He must not only manage, but lead. John Kotter has written that leadership is about handling change, preparing organisations and then managing them as they cope with all the uncertainty and trauma of the new.[4] To lead successfully, he argues, one must do three things: establish a direction by developing a vision of the future and deciding how to get there; align people by communicating and persuading others that what you are proposing makes sense; and finally motivating and inspiring those people to overcome the many hurdles, whether political, bureaucratic or financial, which stand in the path of any change.

> more is expected of a manager than ever

None of this is easy, and requires high degrees of both intellect, to decide on a new strategy and establish an action plan, and human understanding, to bring others along for the ride. But any manager

---

[4] 'What Leaders Really Do', John P. Kotter, *Harvard Business Review*, May–June 1990

wishing to learn and improve his talents should be eager to hurl himself into the very hardest challenge. While it may be tempting to set oneself soft targets and go for the easy wins, it is by dealing with the most gnarly strategic, tactical and human problems that you will learn the most. Over the course of a career, it is the battle-hardened who prove the most agile and successful.

Forcing yourself to adapt early on makes you much less wedded to whatever you might perceive to be your strengths. Studies of high-potential managers whose careers somehow went off track have found that they did so because their initial strengths, such as technical flair or persuasive gifts, eventually became 'fatal flaws' on which they over-relied.[5] Meanwhile those who flourished were those who had been repeatedly forced to retool and learn new skills, to expand their limits and became highly adaptable. This latter group not only underwent dramatic personal change, but they also thought deeply about what they were going through and drew lessons from it. Just going through the trauma is not enough. You have to then sit down and rehash it to extract usable truths.

A fashionable term these days is 'stretch assignment'. People are often told to take on work which stretches them. A more honest way to describe this process would be to say that as a manager you should always be willing to let yourself be smashed into a thousand pieces, in the knowledge that piecing yourself together will make you stronger and better than ever.

It takes real courage to manage one's career like this. To submit to dramatic change, knowing that it contains the possibility for permanent reversal as well as advancement, and then to have the strength to invite critiques of your performance. It all begins with getting a deep and full understanding of yourself.

---

[5] *The Lessons of Experience*, M.W. McCall, M.M. Lombardo and A.M. Morrison, The Free Press, 1988

Chapter 1
Managing yourself

What topics are covered in this chapter?

- Assessing your strengths and weaknesses
- Improving your personal effectiveness
- Tapping into your motivation
- Picking and choosing self-improvement battles
- Pushing yourself to succeed

efore you ask how to manage other people, it is worth pausing to ask how you manage yourself. We are, after all, each our own organisation. We choose how to manage our physical plant; our bodies, our minds, how to invest our time, energies, emotions and financial resources. Whether we recognise it or not, we each have personal balance sheets, made up of varying assets and liabilities, and income statements which measure our progress. We can choose to work late, sacrificing sleep, knowing that the cost of tiredness will have to be paid tomorrow. We can choose to eat or drink more than is good for us, or to rise early and go for that run. We can choose to be testy or patient, fidgety or attentive. We can leave the smart phone in our office, or take it to play with through every meeting.

Understanding how we manage ourselves is the starting point to managing others.

Taking a personal audit

The first step in managing yourself is take an audit of your own life.

Exercise

Take a sheet of paper and record everything you do in the course of an average week. Be specific. Record what time you wake up, how long it takes you to get dressed, have breakfast and drive to work. Do you read the ▶

newspaper at work or at home? What do you listen to during your commute? Then once you're at work, how does your day unfold? Do you plan it? Or are you constantly dealing with the latest crisis? Do you check your email every few seconds, or let it pile up and check it every couple of hours? How do you behave in meetings? What do you do with your notes? Whom do you talk to and for how long? What do you eat for lunch? How long do you spend eating lunch? Once you have this information in front of you, ask yourself two questions. First, are you making the best use of your time? Second, what changes could you make to ensure that you do the most important things to the best of your ability?

The leadership expert Warren Bennis describes the vital role such reflection plays in the life of the manager:

> *Reflecting on experience is a means of having a Socratic dialogue with yourself, asking the right questions at the right time, in order to discover the truth of yourself and your life. What really happened? Why did it happen? What did it do to me? What did it mean to me? In this way, one locates and appropriates the knowledge one needs or, more precisely, recovers what one knew but had forgotten, and becomes, in Goethe's phrase, the hammer rather than the anvil.* [1]

If you want to change, you need to be specific, to monitor and manage yourself as if you were a manufacturing process whose output is your personal success. If you want to give up smoking, it's not enough to rely just on willpower. Willpower is rarely enough. You need to identify those moments when you most want to smoke and plan how you'll best get through them. You must focus on your moments of temptation and seek to change your behaviour at those moments. If it's a cup of morning coffee which makes you hanker for a cigarette, skip the coffee. If it's certain work colleagues who are always dragging you out onto the pavement for a mid-morning cigarette break, know when

---

[1] *On Becoming a Leader,* Warren Bennis, Basic Books, 1989, p. 56

they're coming and disappear. The trick is identifying the triggers for any behaviour you wish to change, whether it is people or environmental cues, and then resisting or avoiding them. Only then can you instil new, better habits.

> identify the trigger for any behaviour you wish to change

To see this in action, consider the Delancey Street Foundation, a remarkable organisation created in San Francisco during the 1970s, to help those who have fallen from the bottom rung of society: thieves, drug addicts, prostitutes and thugs. Many have long criminal records and most have been homeless for years. There are no therapists at the Delancey Street Foundation. The only people there to help you are people a little further in the recovery process than you. The Delancey Street Foundation demands that its residents take care of each other. That they work in businesses together, that they cook and clean together and that they keep an eye on each other's behaviour to ensure that they don't revert to their bad habits. 'These are people who have really hit bottom', says Mimi Silbert, President and CEO. 'They're angry and hopeless . . . and they hate everybody. They hate each other and they hate themselves. But it doesn't matter to us what they've done. We take the people everybody else thinks are losers . . . our only criterion is that they want to change badly enough.'[2] Dr Silbert accepts no more excuses from those who come to Delancey Street, and simply emphasises the importance of new behaviours over everything else, the past included. No sermon or value statement or emotional call to arms comes close to affecting behaviour as much as the constant reinforcement of just a few self-improving behaviours.

Identifying which behaviours to improve depends on who you are. At Delancey Street, the greatest problems are selfishness and confrontation. Gang members come in paranoid and angry, turning even the slightest affront into an explosive fight. The answer? To

---

[2] 'The Mimi Silbert Story', Jerr Boschee and Syl Jones, The Institute for Social Entrepreneurs, 2000

make each resident responsible for another's success. And then to demand that everyone challenges everyone else on every violation.

Even if you have been at the centre for just a week, you are told to be responsible for someone else who has just arrived. From that moment on, you are never asked how you are doing, but how your team is doing.

By demanding her residents watch out for infractions by others and challenge them, Dr Silbert is trying to achieve two things: to force the residents to become more moderate in their language and discussions and to make them accountable for each other.[3] They start to act like an extended family, helping each other out, while also developing their independence through education.

There are so many things an institution like Delancey Street might do. But it chooses to focus on a couple of behaviours and seek to change them, in the belief that they will have a cascading effect on character. As you conduct your personal audit, you should ask what two behaviours, if changed, would have the greatest positive effect on how you live and work? Then focus on them. Don't choose twenty things. You will inevitably fail. Choose just two, record your current behaviour and establish a path to change.

Focusing on what you can control

Optimists are often wrongly defined as people with a positive view of life. It is more accurate to think of them as people with a correct view. If anything goes wrong in their life, they identify why it happened and what they can then do about it. They understand what they can and cannot control, act on that and move on.

A classic model of control is frequently taught to businesses. It lays out three areas of control in both business and in life:

---

[3] *Influencer: The Power to Change Anything*, Kerry Patterson, Joseph Grenny, David Maxfield, Ron McMillan and Al Switzler, McGraw-Hill, 2007

1   Those things you can actually do something about, and you should.

2   Those areas where you are dependent on others. Here, you can try to persuade and influence other people to do what you want, but you cannot force them. You do not have complete control over the outcome.

3   Those factors to which all you can do is respond. You have no control over the weather, or central bank interest rates, the macro-economy or the pace of technological change. But you can respond either effectively or not.

The most effective managers are those with a clear view of these three areas in their own life. They don't waste time trying to change things they can only respond to. That's the work of the office whingers. Instead they do their very best in the areas over which they have control and work to improve their gifts of persuasion and influence to get the bigger things done.

Henry Ford summed up the problem of motivation and work when he said: 'whether you think you can or think you can't, you're right'. He wasn't recommending a moronic, bumpersticker conviction that anyone can do anything provided they put their mind to it. Rather, he was saying that you should start any challenge by defining precisely what you can and cannot do about it, and then resolving to do what is doable. This process of first defining, then setting and confidently working towards goals is what he meant by 'think you can or think you can't'. The right attitude plus realistic goal-setting was his definition of success.

Even the slightest hesitancy or doubt can be extremely detrimental. As one management slogan puts it, '99 per cent is a bitch, 100 per cent is a breeze'.[4] Total commitment to a task makes it easy, by comparison with 99 per cent commitment, which can lead to all kinds of conflicts and delays. Think of those people in your life

---

[4] *Workarounds that Work*, Russell Bishop, McGraw-Hill, 2011, p. 19

who are completely committed to a couple of priorities, their work and their families perhaps. Then consider those who are pulled in a thousand different directions because they have never fully committed to any.

So as part of that initial audit, break your work down into those areas where you can make a difference without anyone's help and then start there. Work, like exercise, begets more work. The more you do, the more you want to do, as each small high of achievement inspires the need for another. Make a list of all your daily routines and potential tasks and put them in separate buckets. Which ones should you start? Which should you cut out of your life? And which should you continue doing more or less of?

> break your work down into areas where you can make a difference without anyone's help

De-cluttering

Lew Wasserman, a Hollywood mogul who began his professional life as an agent, used to wait in his office until everyone had gone home and then walk around looking for papers left on his employees' desks. If he found them he would sweep them into the bin. A messy desk, he thought, implied a messy mind.

Personal organisation is the weight loss industry of business. Everyone wants it and everyone knows how to achieve it. But we are always looking for the next gizmo or system which promises to make it easier, from Filofaxes to iPhones. But just as we know the answer to weight loss, eating less and exercising more, so we know the key to personal productivity. Do more by doing less. It sounds rather Zen, but the idea is simple. The most successful professional lives are those which are highly focused. They are not a cacophony of conflicting obligations, impossible deadlines and political machinations. They involve the streamlined pursuit of a single goal.

Apple's success after Steve Jobs returned as CEO in 1997 might be reduced to a single idea: making the complex simple. For a company so big, Apple's product line under Jobs remained small: Macs, iPod, iPhone, iPad and iTunes, with a few variations on each theme. Jobs's clarity of thought and purpose was reflected in his dress, the jeans and black turtleneck, his car, always German, always silver, even his household appliances. Jobs once explained the process for choosing his washing machine. He and his family were dissatisfied with their American machine. So they spent two weeks discussing the problem over dinner. They talked about design, function, water usage and environmental impact and finally decided on buying appliances from the German manufacturer Miele.[5] Imagine how many distractions you have banished from your life if you can focus so intently on buying a washing machine.

For most of us, our days are more like splat-the-rat, flailing at problems as they emerge, hoping that one good wallop does the trick, but fearing that nothing is ever well and truly solved. Multitasking is a term for it. It often seems that the division between those who choose to focus on one task at a time and those who multitask is a theological one, each side claiming to be more productive.

Academic research, however, suggests that the relationship between multitasking and productivity follows an upside-down U-curve. A little multitasking improves our productivity. But then we plateau and too much multitasking, too much work and too many relationships to manage, slows us down. We would be better off taking the Jobs washing machine approach: taking a problem, solving it once and for all and then moving on.

People who move house have a common dream. That their moving truck will simply disappear along with all their stuff and that they will be able to start afresh. Which manager does not crave that elusive sense of mental lightness: the clean break, the

---

[5] 'Steve Jobs: The Next Insanely Great Thing', Gary Wolf, *Wired*, February 1996

clean desk, the same old problems finally dealt with and only new opportunities ahead?

Wasserman tried to impose it with his nightly desk purges. But that's not the only way. The late English writer Patrick Leigh Fermor found a different path in his book, *A Time to Keep Silence*, when he went on retreat to the Abbey of Saint-Wandrille de Fontanelle in northern France. At first he was frustrated by the silence and inaction, his mind still racing at city speed. Then he was overcome by tiredness and slept longer than ever before. Finally he reached a state 'full of energy and limpid freshness'. His 'desire for talk, movement and nervous expression' had 'languished and finally died for lack of any stimulus or nourishment' among the monks. By the end of his stay, he was in that state every manager wants to be, free of the 'hundred anxious trivialities that poison everyday life' and suddenly more productive than ever.

Blake Mycoskie, the founder of TOMS Shoes, a San Francisco-based company which donates one pair of shoes to the poor for every pair it sells, recommends that when starting a new venture you should remove everything extraneous from your life. Wear different versions of the same outfit every day. Decide on a healthy diet and stick to it, so you're not one of those people in the lunch line agonising over what to choose. Make your personal finances as simple as possible. Reduce your commute. Chuck out all those ties and shoes you never wear and keep just the ones you need. Outsource everything you can so that you can focus on what really matters in your life.

Not everyone will be capable of such a radical de-cluttering. If you have a family, there will always be bikes in the garage and clothes piled up on the floor. We cannot all live lives of monastic simplicity and devotion to work. There is always more to life than that.

But efficiency experts do recommend certain basic actions:

- Make lists so that you can free your mind of the burden of having to remember what you need to do. Then check off items on the list as you go. Simply jotting down everything which is rolling around your head is another useful process. All those long-buried ideas and ambitions.

- Take an inventory of them and discard those which are impossible or outlived and focus on those you can do something about. It will stop your mind looping endlessly around the same stale problems just when you are trying to sleep.

- Keep your desk free of paperwork.

- Keep your in-box empty by dealing with things as they arise or in concentrated, scheduled bursts rather than letting them pile up.

These techniques do not change who you are, but they can have a powerful effect on how much you can get done.[6]

Taking care of yourself

It may seem personally intrusive for a management book to recommend getting more sleep, and yet it is hard to imagine a manager doing his best if constantly frazzled. An ambitious manager must be constantly aware of challenges to his physical well-being and ready to fight them off. Sleep, nutrition, fitness and rest are not just health issues. They have a direct effect on your ability to manage effectively.

Buddhists say of meditation that it is an attempt to control the 'wild horses of the mind'. For the manager, wild horses, in the form of distractions, are ubiquitous. There are always phones ringing, text message alerts flashing, meetings to go to, people wanting five minutes of your time. But it is vital, if you are to get

> wild horses, in the form of distractions, are ubiquitous

---

[6] *Getting Things Done*, David Allen, Piatkus, 2002

anything done, to manage your capacity to focus, to give the big problems your complete attention. Distractions are the termites of management, capable of turning the greatest talents and organisations to dust. Lists are a great way to attack the problem.

Tony Schwartz, the author of *Be Excellent at Anything*, recommends we examine ourselves as a professional athlete would. We are not computers, after all, designed to run several different programs at top speed continuously. 'Human beings', says Schwartz, 'are designed to be rhythmic'. We have pulses and muscles which quicken and slow, expand and contract. Our energy hits peaks and troughs during each day. We do best when we focus on a task intensely for 90 minutes and then take a break, a brisk walk or even a nap. Companies may frown on employees napping, but it makes a huge difference to productivity. Churchill was a frequent cat-napper and it enabled him to put in yeoman hours during the Second World War. He also worked at a lectern, believing he thought more sharply while standing up.

Schwartz maintains that if a 'person works continuously through the day, she'll produce less than a person of equal talent who works very intensely for short periods and then recovers before working intensely again'.

As a manager you should bear this in mind when you look at how you work, and what you expect of others. Would you be cross to see an employee napping after lunch? Or delighted to see them taking such good care to maximise their productivity? Do you view employees as commodities, to be acquired and depleted, or as assets to be invested in for long-term growth?

Being effective

Another beneficial routine is to identify when in the day you are most effective, and clear that time to do the most important task of the day. For most of us, that time will be first thing in the morning.

And yet what do most people do first thing? Clutter their minds by opening their email or reading the paper, thereby turning their time and attention over to others. You should take advantage of those times when your mind is most fresh, eliminate all that is unnecessary and get the biggest task of each day accomplished. Answering email may feel good. At least you have accomplished something. But it is a short-term sugar rush compared to the full, healthy meal of attacking a real problem and finding a solution. Researchers have found that breaking away from work to answer just a single quick email takes up 15 minutes of the day in terms of lost concentration.

Again, all of this takes discipline. To change your morning routine so that you are left alone to concentrate on your work, not the concerns of others. To take a pillow into work and not feel guilty about taking a nap. To create a system of personal management which allows you to operate at your very highest level.

Finding your motivation

A further part of this personal audit will involve asking yourself why you do what you do. It is easy to laugh at corporate mission statements, with their vacuous phrasing and lofty ambitions. But their intention is admirable. Unless you know why you do what you do, you will have a hard time convincing others they should follow you. You might be doing the work because you find it intrinsically fascinating, or because it provides a life and rewards for your family.

Whatever it is, you need to identify it and keep it at the front of your mind, to avoid those lethal moments when you sit in your chair as night falls and the cleaners arrive at the office and you stare at the framed photograph of your boyfriend or your children and ask yourself: what am I doing here?

Many people analyse their career as if it were a business opportunity. They seek out growing markets for their products or services, they look at compensation and the sustainability of a particular company or sector. But the fact is none of these will ensure that you do your best work.

The former US President Calvin Coolidge was once asked about the secret of success and he replied: 'Nothing in the world can take the place of persistence. Talent will not; nothing is more common than unsuccessful men with talent. Genius will not; unrewarded genius is almost a proverb. Education will not; the world is full of educated derelicts. Persistence and determination alone are omnipotent.'

We all know 'unsuccessful men with talent' or 'educated derelicts'. But how do we avoid joining their ranks? The key, according to Coolidge, is to find work you enjoy so much you are ready to work hard at it. Liking your work, and especially the people it brings you into contact with, is not just a privilege for the fortunate. It determines how fully you will live your life.

People often respond to this point by asking, but how do I find out what I like? The answer to what you like is not a specific job but a set of conditions. One recommended method for discovering these is to admit to your 'evil secrets'.[7] What don't you like to admit about yourself? For example, if you say, 'I don't like to admit it, but I hate working with other people', then you need to find a situation where you work alone. If your evil secret is that you like showing off how clever you are, then find a place which welcomes that kind of behaviour. You could also draft a list of your most recent work and find which people and situations gave you the most pleasure and seek out more of them.

One way to think of personal success is to break it down into four components:

● Happiness

● Achievement

---

[7] 'Go For What You Really Want', David Maister, *Legal Business*, January 1996

- Significance
- Legacy.[8]

Our tendency is to focus on only one component at a time. We scramble for a better title or higher salary and ignore its significance, or the positive effect it might have on others. We strive to leave a legacy which will enable others to succeed in the future, and in the process forgo our own happiness.

> we strive to leave a legacy to enable others to succeed in the future

This model is useful because it accommodates different perceptions of success. A landscaper who spends all day trimming hedges and mowing lawns may have a very different view of success from a management consultant who revels in his Air Miles elite status and the constant vibration of his BlackBerry. A grandparent may view success very differently from her granddaughter who is just starting out at an investment bank. But if you can assign each of your actions to one of the four components of success, and try to keep some sort of balance, you will be well on your way to a lifetime of success.

For example, most of us want to have successful professional and personal lives. We wish to achieve great things and be happy. But great achievement requires hard work, much of which may be tiring or tedious. It is not always consistent with happiness. Similarly, taking the time to do something significant, such as helping a friend with a personal problem, may not fit with your desire to put in more hours at work. The trick then is to see each action for what it is, assign it the proper label and see where you are in each category.

The truly successful person is constantly moving between the components, doing something for achievement's sake one

---

[8] 'Success that Lasts', Laura Nash and Howard Stevenson, *Harvard Business Review*, February 2004

moment, and for legacy's sake another, cheering up a friend over breakfast, then playing tennis for himself in the evening, always seeking to keep the four buckets as full as possible. Only taken together do they make up success.

Managers can apply this idea to their businesses as well as to themselves. They can seek to ensure their employees' happiness by creating enough space for them to enjoy each day. They can examine financial performance to see if it is directly linked to meaningful work or simply the result of some gimmicky accounting. Significance will depend on creating products and services of real value, and legacy is about preparing your organisation for the future.

Knowing yourself

Personal relationships are an inevitable part of management. Whether you like it or not, people will judge you as much as what you produce. Your ability to lead and persuade will depend on so called 'soft' issues, such as how likeable you are and how trustworthy. If you have poor relationships with your bosses, your peers or those reporting to you, you will most likely be an ineffective manager.

Exercise

We will return to this challenge in Chapter 2, but in this chapter on managing yourself, it is right to ask whether you have any idea how people perceive you. Have you ever asked? And what are your own behaviours? How do you react to criticism, for example? Do you fight back, crumple or go away and reflect? If your boss challenges you, are your reactions driven by an attitude of antagonism or dependence? First write down three adjectives which you think describe you. Then reflect on three memorable situations at work: one where you succeeded, one where you failed, and one where you were left feeling uncertain how you had done. Be honest about the causes and effects of each situation. This should cover no more than a single sheet of paper. Ask ▶

yourself this: does the way you think of yourself match how you felt in these three situations?

Some managers are in constant conflict with their bosses, regarding them as obstacles to their own ascent, or people removed from the reality of the business. Others swallow everything their boss says as gospel and refuse to tell the truth for fear of causing offence or damaging their own career prospects. Neither position is especially healthy, but many managers fall into one or other category. Changing these attitudes may even require therapy, as they often have deep psychological roots, but recognising them is a good first step. It will go a long way to explaining your successes or failures at work.

Ideally, a boss should be someone who provides clear expectations, gives you the tools to do your best work, and responds fairly to your successes and failures. Every employee is entitled to hold their boss to this standard.

Managing demands that you find a way to be compatible with many different working styles. You could try to force everyone to conform to your own, but it will be impossible. Instead, you will have to find ways to make do, to find areas of agreement, to compromise on working habits or how you express yourself. You will have employees who respond to coaxing and others who spring to life when threatened. You will have bosses who micromanage and others who are aloof, some who are susceptible to flattery, others who loathe it. Some will make their expectations clear, others will expect you to deduce them. There will be colleagues who like to be kept informed of everything, others who want only the highlights. Adapting to these different styles is not giving in or sacrificing your personality. It is how all of us get through life and get things done.

So take a good look at yourself. Ask your friends and family and anyone else you trust to give you an honest assessment of how they see you. Small things matter. When most people think about you, they will tend to remember the worst and most recent things you did. They will remember the one moment you were abusive and angry, not the ten others when you were pure sunshine. Those moments come to define who you are. Figuring out what you can and cannot change is the first task of the effective manager.

Adaptation is a vital managerial skill. But so is knowing your strengths and weaknesses and those of others, and realising what is easily changed and what is not.

Working with what you've got[9]

One of the paradoxes of leadership is that the people who most want to lead are often the last people we would want to be given the responsibility. The pushy hack, the selfish careerist and the ruthless opportunist are just some of the unpleasant types who tend to force their way to the top. They thrive in hyper-competitive environments. Decent people, who might actually make better leaders, seem to have a harder time scrambling upwards. They may have exactly what it takes to lead, but lack what it takes to get the chance.

But it would be wrong to let such stereotypes determine your behaviour.

One way academics have sought to categorise the character traits required to succeed has been to divide us all into extroverts and

---

[9] Parts of this section are taken from Delves Broughton, P., 'Leadership is not just for the extraverts', *The Financial Times*, 29 November 2010. © The Financial Times Limited 2010. All rights reserved. For the full article, see the appendix at the back of the book.

introverts, and much research has found that it is the extroverts who do best. Extroverts like to be the centre of attention, seek status and approval and talk a lot in social settings. They are good at motivating employees and leading change. Consequently, they earn more and get more promotions.

So what if you decided after all this personal auditing, reflection and feedback that you're not an extrovert? Are you done for as a manager? Fortunately not. More important than the degree to which you are introverted or extroverted is how your employees react to you.[10] If employees are passive, an extrovert thrives by giving a clear lead. If employees are more proactive, the introvert does better because he actually listens and incorporates their advice into his decision making.

> with employees who are more proactive, the introvert does better because he listens

This finding arose from an academic study of a chain of pizza restaurants, which looked at financial performance and the nature of the managers and employees, and a laboratory experiment in which people were asked to act either extroverted or introverted in managing a group folding T-shirts. The evidence came back clearly that a proactive group either butted heads or felt under-appreciated working for an extrovert leader and performed better under an introvert. The passive groups worked best for an extrovert and felt lost under an introvert. It is a great example of advances in management science turning conventional wisdom upside down.

The advice for introverts in business has generally been to be more extroverted, to follow the old salesman's mantra, 'act enthusiastic to be enthusiastic'. But many forced grins later, we are finding that

---

[10] 'Reversing the Extroverted Leadership Advantage: The Role of Employee Proactivity', Adam Grant, Francesca Gino and David Hoffman, *The Academy of Management Journal*, Vol. 54, 2011

doesn't need to be the case. It is clearly not necessary to be the life and soul of a party in order to run a great business.

Bill Gates of Microsoft and Mark Zuckerberg of Facebook are neither natural glad-handers nor extroverts, but they have the bullheadedness and genius that drags others along. Anna Wintour, the British editor of American *Vogue*, and Giorgio Armani are frosty characters who are nonetheless accomplished managers in a highly creative industry. Sir Richard Branson, the founder of The Virgin Group, has turned himself into an extrovert for the public but is said to be an introvert in private.

Introverts it turns out have always done well at engineering and accounting companies, which tend to emphasise technical skills over personality. But other industries, especially those where conditions change quickly and dramatically, could benefit from hiring, valuing and promoting more introverts. Extrovert leaders might succeed in these environments, but it's rather like putting all your money on a single number on the roulette wheel. Far better to have an introvert leader ready to absorb a lot of input in order to discover the best processes or business models.

To get to become leaders, introverts must still prove themselves terrific individual contributors. Without the noise and flash of the extrovert, they will have to find subtler ways to show they can lead. But once in a leadership or managerial position, they no longer need to worry about loosening up at parties and becoming more extroverted.

Instead, they can succeed by surrounding themselves with proactive employees, and giving them the autonomy and respon-sibility they require to perform at their best. They can focus on encouraging behaviour that complements their existing style rather than trying to acquire an awkward new one.

The lesson here is that before you try to turn yourself into someone you are not, it is worth discovering whether your supposed weaknesses can be turned into a strength. Only an honest assessment of who you are can get you to this position.

Combating performance anxiety

Equally, it is worth remembering that almost any personal problem can be fixed. It is quite common for people to say 'oh, I'm not good at this or that' and then assume that it is too late to change, when in fact many problems can at least be alleviated, if not cured.

Take performance anxiety. It is a situation we have all witnessed or experienced first-hand. The make-or-break moment arrives. The decisive shot, the well-rehearsed concert performance, the public speech. Then suddenly – aaarggh. It all goes wrong. The ball whistles past, the fingers slide all over the keyboard, the voice becomes an inarticulate mumble. You are now a choker. You have failed in the clutch.

It is an unfortunate truth that years of patient success can so easily be undone. Ask Greg Norman, the Australian-born golfer, who collapsed so spectacularly in the 1996 Masters tournament, blowing a comfortable lead on his final round and losing by five strokes. Or Alex Rodriguez, the New York Yankees slugger, whose epic regular-season statistics were for years undermined by his reputation as a serial big-game choker.

It is not just mere mortals who suffer it, sweating out the Sunday night before a Monday morning presentation at work. Great athletes and musicians suffer just as much. The difference is that they have found a way to cope.

Polls that investigate such things reveal that public speaking is one of our greatest fears. More frightening than spiders or heights. The terror of exposure and humiliation in front of others – of flubbing one's lines or saying the wrong thing, of dropping the

public speaking is one of our greatest fears

microphone or being plain boring – is enough to provoke midnight shakes in people who otherwise bounce unaffected through life.

And yet, when you examine it from the audience's perspective, what's to be scared of? Scientists once conducted an experiment in which heart-rate monitors were strapped to students as they listened to various lectures. Their heart rate peaked at the start of the lectures and then steadily declined.[11] Regardless of how good the lecture, the human body's tendency is to slow down when sitting through a talk, and our minds then follow.

For the vast majority of speeches, audience expectations are low to nonexistent – for the simple fact that most speeches are boring and most speakers talentless. We listen because of the speaker more than the speech. We listen to politicians and CEOs because they are powerful, to actors or writers because they are famous. Now and then, we hear someone who actually manages to engage us, but often our interest has a lot to do with the moment or the context. Churchill's great wartime speeches are remembered as much for the time at which he gave them as what he actually said.

So the first thought for anyone scared of public speaking should be this: take no risks and be boring. The worst you'll do is meet expectations. If you're even mildly interesting, you're a winner. If you're actually engaging, you are a rare breed. There are also all kinds of things you can do if you suffer from stage fright. You can arrive early and make sure you have back-up copies of your speech. There are any number of books to help you craft better speeches. *The Penguin Book of Twentieth-Century Speeches* is an excellent greatest hits collection.

You can seek to control all that is controllable about the situation. If only 10 people show up in a 1000-person auditorium, you can get them all together at the front and sit on the edge of a stage to turn an embarrassment into an intimate seminar. In order to improve, you

---

[11] *Confessions of a Public Speaker*, Scott Berkun, O'Reilly, 2011

must seek out honest feedback. No one in an audience will ever tell a speaker anything other than some version of 'that was great'. To improve, you need to video yourself and review the tape mercilessly, or ask for anonymous written responses from the audience.

Equally, you should assess your own moments of greatest anxiety. What provoked them? Were you being realistic? People who suffer from this kind of social anxiety are often misreading other people's signals. They see someone yawn and instantly assume their speech is boring, rather than that the yawner was out late the night before. They hear someone laugh, and imagine they have made a fool of themselves, when in fact they have simply provoked a humorous memory in a member of their audience. Focusing on these moments and reframing them in your mind takes conscious effort, but it is the basis of overcoming these specific worries. The good news is such worries can be overcome. Social anxieties tend to be quite narrow. People who fear public speaking may be quite comfortable at a dinner party. Likewise a party wallflower can light up on stage. The only way to change your response to situations you fear is to study your behaviour in microscopic detail and

> you have to abandon your pride to be this honest with yourself

ask at every turn: are my fears rational? You have to abandon your pride to be this honest with yourself.

One of the most notorious corporate presentations in recent memory was delivered at a conference by Steve Ballmer, the chief executive of Microsoft. The relevant parts are easily viewable online. A huge man, Mr Ballmer bursts into the room, leaps onto the stage, wide sweat patches visible on his shirt, and screams like a bee-stung grizzly: 'Come on! Give it up for me!'

It is a kind of 'CEO's gone wild' moment and should be a warning to anyone mulling an extra Red Bull before appearing in public. But it should also provide reassurance to the nervous. If this man can act like this and remain CEO of one of the world's largest corporations, then there is hope for us all.

Even if you prepare well and avoid disaster, of course, you may not charm everyone in the audience. But you can at least avoid being cripplingly nervous before that lunch-time presentation and wishing it were tomorrow.

Scholars of 'choking' say there are six traits that help people pull off a clutch performance:

- Focus
- Discipline
- Adaptability
- Presence (i.e. actual involvement in the task at hand)
- Fear
- Desire.

All of these revolve around the central concept of putting things in perspective, realising your own talents and limitations, not exaggerating or underestimating the importance of the situation, focusing on the moment and what you can control, rather than some larger unmanageable set of circumstances.[12]

Studies of golfers who choke find that the later they pick up the sport, the more likely they are to choke.[13] The later you learn, it seems, the more dependent you are on your working memory, or rather, you over-think the game. The younger you learn, the more you develop your skills using sensory and motor-brain areas. Thus when you are bent over that game-winning putt, you just play your stroke and don't worry the ball away from the cup. Similarly, in maths tests, people best suited to problem solving, reasoning and comprehension are the most likely to fail under the pressure of a timed exam. Part of the reason is that they are not inclined to take

---

[12] *Choke: What the Secrets of the Brain Reveal about Getting It Right when You Have to*, Sian Beilock, Constable, 2011

[13] *Clutch: Why Some People Excel under Pressure and Others Don't*, Paul Sullivan, Portfolio, 2010

short cuts to answers. They are also prone to putting far too much meaning into situations they deem important. Their reasoning quickly becomes worrying, which in turn takes over their brain, leaving little room for much else. This question of when to reason and when to go with intuition will crop up time and again for managers. It always pays to go as far as you can with analysis and reason, but at some point, a well-honed intuition can cut through a good deal of noise and lead to inspired and decisive action.

Another classic problem is when individuals start to worry too much about the broader significance of an important moment rather than focusing on what needs to be done in the present. For years, Alex Rodriguez, the highest-paid baseball player of his era and by many measures the best, would fail in crucial situations. It seemed as though that when great things were asked of him, he would be overcome by the fear of criticism and his constant mental comparisons of himself with the greatest legends of baseball. He wanted so much to seize these moments and have himself compared to baseball's immortals that it choked him up. It was only later in his career, after his marriage had dissolved and he had spent months recovering from an ailing hip that he discovered the humility needed to be a clutch player. As he described it: 'For me, with no expecta-tions and trusting my teammates and taking the walks and doing the little things, you end up doing big things.' Finally, he found a way to focus on the moment.

Managers can apply similar lessons of careful and repeated practice; writing down your worries to make them explicit and to stop them distracting you under stress; and not worrying about what you cannot control. Athletes are often told that in pressure situations, they should try to distract themselves so that they don't over-think their mechanics; keep a steady rhythm; and change their technique every so often to stay fresh. But perhaps

> there is value in putting yourself in stressful situations

most important of all – in business, sports and a good deal else in life – there is value in putting yourself in stressful situations so that you learn how to handle them better. The more we perform in the clutch, the less likely we are to choke.

Trusting your own judgement[14]

The phrase 'paradigm shift' should be enough to send chills down any manager's spine. It is what consultants say when they don't know what else to recommend. Or economists, when all their predictions have just gone up in smoke. 'What you need now, dear client, is a "paradigm shift". Here's my bill and I'll be off.'

But since the failure of many financial institutions to predict or manage through the economic crisis which began in 2008, this is what many economists and business academics are calling for: a 'paradigm shift' in how we think about the balance between human judgement and the efficiency of scale in running a profitable business. Banks have been accused of a 'judgement deficit' relying on black box computer models rather than human beings. Economists blamed markets and regulators for placing too much faith in the efficient markets hypothesis and assuming that market prices reflected fully all relevant information.[15]

What is missing from this debate is the voice of the manager, the person who more than any economist or academic, understands this problem intuitively. Because in any business, large or small, financial crisis or none, this problem comes up every single day. Do you prefer to trust people or processes in running your business? In difficult moments, do you put your faith in the

---

[14] Parts of this section are taken from Delves Broughton, P., 'Nothing beats the exercise of judgement', *The Financial Times*, 6 September 2010. © The Financial Times Limited 2010. All rights reserved. For the full article, please see the appendix at the back of the book.

[15] 'Needed: A New Economic Paradigm', Joseph Stiglitz, *Financial Times*, 19 August 2010

seemingly clean, dependable data or the executive who says she feels uneasy about the decision the data is leading to?

A few years ago, economists were briefly fascinated by the distinction between hard and soft information. Hard information includes numbers, charts and empirical data. Soft information includes intuition, or personal judgements about people and situations. The great investor George Soros once said that he knows it is time to sell an asset when his lower back starts to ache. That's the soft signal that might support a hard judgement on whether it is better to own, say, the euro or the dollar.

In hiring, a CV contains hard information about degrees obtained and jobs done. Personal references are the soft stuff, which help an employer distinguish between the blithering gasbag with blue chip degrees and the diligent genius with only a high-school education. All big decisions require a balance of soft and hard information.

The other part of this problem is how you grow. Businesses requiring endless individual judgements are not nearly as scalable as those built on technology platforms. The reason banks came to depend on credit scores to make loans was that it simplified the process to the point where they could make more loans, faster, with what seemed like a satisfactory level of scrutiny.

The blow-ups of the financial crisis aside, it's hard to see this model fundamentally changing. Some may pine for the traditional bank manager tyrannising a local lending system, but the efficiency and profitability of scale lending is not going away. Furthermore, it's not as though depending on soft information in finance is any protection against disaster. The success of micro-lending in the developing world may seem to justify extending credit based on soft information, the observation that people without any financial history will work hard to fulfil their obligations to their families and communities.

But then Bernie Madoff's scam was a victory of soft over hard information. The whispered remark in Palm Beach, 'this Madoff's a genius', was valued more than any proper look at what Madoff was doing. The slow growth of person-to-person lending may in part be because most of us still value the impersonal lending processes of large institutions.

Bo Burlingham's excellent book, *Small Giants – Companies that Choose to be Great instead of Big*, describes several US companies that faced similar challenges to the ones that economists are now debating. Given the opportunity to become bigger, do you seize it? Or is there something magical about staying small? What are the pitfalls of size? At what point does a manager go from being a manager of people to an implementer of organisational processes? And what gets lost if that happens?

I know the chief executive of a Midwestern company with 90 employees who believes firmly that going beyond that would change the nature of the company for the worse. He frets that his employees would lose their sense of purpose, the sense that their work and the decisions they make matter. It means passing up opportunities to scale what he does, but he believes that preserving the human dimension of his company is worth it.

This is not to say there is virtue in staying small. But rather that for the right manager and company, there is value – just as there is value for others in being large. It comes down to what economists struggle to model and managers grapple with all day: judgement. No paradigm shift required.

Doing what feels right[16]

In 2010, two films were released which painted very dark pictures of business success. In *Money Never Sleeps*, the sequel to *Wall*

---

[16] Parts of this section are taken from Delves Broughton, P., 'The Hollywood boss is no work of fiction', *The Financial Times*, 10 September 2010. © The Financial Times Limited 2010. All rights reserved. For the full article, please see the appendix at the back of the book.

Street, the fallen Wall Street financier Gordon Gekko tells us that 'idealism kills deals'. It is the most pungent line in the film, and a bracing rejoinder to anyone who argues that business is about 'doing well by doing good'. In fact, the whole film, like the original, is a perverse homage to appalling behaviour. Then came *The Social Network*, about Mark Zuckerberg and the founding of Facebook. Mr Zuckerberg is not just portrayed as ambitious, a reasonable trait in the founder of a start-up, but also as vengeful, vicious, duplicitous and devoid of even the most basic social skills.

Zuckerberg's story, as told in the film, is quite familiar to anyone who has studied the history of the technology industry since the 1970s. The young Bill Gates, by most accounts, was a similar kind of nightmare, screaming at his staff and elbowing aggressively past rivals as he built Microsoft. When he founded Apple, Steve Jobs was said to push his developers to work ungodly hours and to treat both colleagues and competitors with contempt.

And yet how much of this makes it into the management books? Where is the guru who tells us that the way to get the most out of an organisation is to ratchet up the pressure until everyone is desperate and frazzled? And then to run psychological rings round them? Why is it left to Hollywood to tell us what we already know, that those who succeed in business are not always the most likeable people? That to succeed on the epic scale of a Zuckerberg, Gates or Gekko, may require some deeply unpalatable traits?

> why is it left to Hollywood to tell us what we already know?

What is the ordinary manager to make of it all? There you sit in a negotiation seminar learning about creating 'win–win' situations, while part of you suspects that, as one corporate lawyer once put it to me, 'the only win–win situation is one where the same person wins twice'. There you are downloading the latest rules on diversity and sexual harassment, while Mr Zuckerberg, whose venture before

Facebook was a website that invited users to rank female students at Harvard by physical attractiveness, rockets past towards billions.

In *Hardball: Are You Playing to Play or Playing to Win?*, one of the few books to address this issue of business's dark side, George Stalk and Rob Lachenauer, two consultants at Boston Consulting Group, wrote: 'Winners in business play rough and don't apologise'. They argued that hardball is not about breaking the law or cheating, but about relentless competition, bordering on brutality, and absolute clarity of purpose. It is certainly not about 'people skills'.

The *Hardball* way lists five 'fundamental behaviors of winning': 'focus relentlessly on competitive advantage'; 'strive for extreme competitive advantage', don't be happy just being better at something, but try to be much, much better; 'avoid attacking directly', because unless you have overwhelming force, you are better off being sneaky; 'exploit people's will to win', by motivating them to become slavering, hyper-competitive beasts; and 'know the caution zone', play to the edges of the pitch, but not beyond.

They then list five strategies to be deployed in 'bursts of ruthless intensity'. These are: 'devastate rivals' profit sanctuaries'; 'plagiarize with pride'; 'deceive the competition'; 'unleash massive and overwhelming force' once you have it; and 'raise competitors' costs', the final turn of the ratchet after you have destroyed their profits, copied, tricked and beaten them unconscious.

'Hardball is tough, not sadistic', they write. 'Yes, you want rivals to squirm, but not so visibly that you are viewed as a bully. In fact, you want the people in your world – the same ones you demand straight answers from – to cheer you on. And many of them will, as they share the riches your strategies generate.'

Fail at hardball, or its more extreme derivations, and you may not even have the consolation of having fought a decent fight. But succeed, and you will have all the resources in the world to buy your way to redemption – however Hollywood depicts you.

This is in direct opposition to the emphasis on emotional intelligence and the so-called 'soft skills' such as listening, caring and showing empathy.

Hardball has always gone on at the highest levels of business and politics. Even those with public reputations for being sensitive, decent types often employ sidekicks to body-check, tackle and hurt. Tony Blair had Alastair Campbell. Barack Obama's first White House chief of staff, Rahm Emanuel, was a notorious hard nut and compulsive curser. As Obama said in a speech one Mother's Day, 'This is a tough holiday for Rahm Emanuel because he's not used to saying the word "day" after "mother".' Obama could have polish and style because he had Emanuel knee-capping in the back room. It harked back to another President, Richard Nixon, who once said: 'People react to fear, not love. They don't teach that in Sunday school but it's true.'

Everyone knows that the great fortunes and innovations of this world are rarely created by cuddly, honourable people. They are created by egotists, bullies and liars. Spend too much time mollycoddling your employees and you will be overtaken by someone who does not. For an employee, the cost of working for these monsters is balanced by the reward of association with a winner who won't have to fire them.

In tough times, you want a leader like General George Patton, who used to practise his general's face in the mirror each morning to make sure he would look imposing enough to his troops. You want someone to scowl and object and argue in negotiations on your behalf, not roll over to keep everyone happy. And most people know that their best work is not coaxed gently from them but dragged out under extreme pressure, intimidation and raw fear.

During boom times, we hear a lot about 'doing well by doing good', of how profit and compassion are compatible ideas. In the United States, a firm which tracks emotional intelligence in the workplace reported that in 2010, for the first time since 2003, the tendency of employees to understand others had declined. People suffering from stress brought on by the recession have little time for other people and their problems.

It is easy to see the perils of practising hardball, the risks of being loathed and derided. Harvey Weinstein, the film producer, has been a notorious hardballer, shouting and intimidating his way to the top. But hundreds of millions of dollars and multiple Oscars later, he has triumphed in an industry with minuscule odds of success. Bill Gates is now as tough on issues of global health as he was developing Windows. If you are an African with malaria, this is tremendous news. Who would not want Bill Gates turning his attention to their problem? He will fix it. And success, whatever it took to achieve it, earns a lot of forgiveness.

The only way through this conundrum is to do what feels right to you. There are natural hardballers and natural empathisers. There are those who play hardball and do nothing but alienate their employees, colleagues and customers, and fail in the process. Equally, there are managers who pay attention and show kindness and are rewarded with loyalty in even the toughest situations. The only habit guaranteed to fail is being phoney.

Moving the flywheel of success

Careers obey the most basic laws of physics. First you need to get them moving, and only then can you begin to steer. An immobile object is much harder to direct. The process of getting things started is rarely pretty. Friends and family may disagree on your professional choices. Even you might be hesitant. Watching a career gain momentum, it can look less like someone turning on the ignition in a brand new BMW, and more like a man trying to push several bales of hay across a crowded car park. But with any luck, the indignities and difficulties of this process won't have to be repeated again and again throughout your career.

> careers obey the most basic laws of physics

The ideal job, like a pair of new shoes, should be uncomfortable at the start, as it should allow room for you to grow. If it's too easy, you will learn nothing, and though you may do well to start with, you will soon get bored. If it's too hard, you will fail. Ideally, you should be able to envisage a situation in which within four to six months, you will be producing decent results. Picking such a job requires you to analyse its requirements and your capabilities. If the gap is too wide, you should forget it. If the fit is too perfect, perhaps you need something more challenging. This applies especially early in a managerial career when you are seeking to prove to others what you can do.

If you do make the right choices early on and put yourself in a position where you can develop relationships, develop expertise and prove yourself capable, you will set in motion the flywheel of success. The more people who know you and trust you, the more opportunities you will get, and assuming you keep doing what is asked of you, the higher you will rise, accumulating responsibility and power.

One of the greatest mistakes any aspiring manager can make is to hoard his talent rather than taking risks with it. The great advantage of a stretch assignment is that it offers much higher returns on an investment of talent than ordinary, humdrum work. If you are asked to do something challenging, the odds are your company is paying particular attention to how you do and assigning special resources to it. Succeed, and it will be as if someone has attached a turbo-booster to your career. And once again, the higher you go, the more people you will meet who will help advance your career, assign you responsibility and invest their fortunes in yours. Such is the nature of power.

And power is very different from mere titles or salary. A young person who serves at the elbow of a senior executive and impresses him, despite a lowly title and meagre salary, may have much more power than a well-paid though sidelined vice president. Equally, someone who is a master of what they do at a lower level may wield more power in certain situations than a senior figure who is chasing after his work like a man chasing his hat down a windy street. To keep the flywheel of success moving fast, you will have to demonstrate mastery at the same time as moving close to the powerful heart of your organisation, regardless of whatever titles or pay is promised in the short term.

As with any risk-taking, to make a risky investment with your career is not always an easy choice. To accept a job overseas, far from headquarters, may not only demand you learn a new language and live far from family and friends, but it may end up excluding you from the rat race at home. But it may equally give you the chance to manage several divisions and functions, to open up a new market, and acquire the kind of varied, executive experience it might have taken years to acquire back home.

Perhaps the best way to minimise such risks, aside from actually doing your job well, is to ensure you have a good network of relationships within and without your organisation. You need mentors who understand what you are doing, believe in you and will help you if your risk turns out badly. You need colleagues who will welcome you back and put your career back on track. A network like this is vital not only in terms of lubricating your day-to-day activities, but it can be either the trampoline, vaulting you higher than you imagine, or the safety net, protecting you if you fall in the course of your managerial career.

Top 10 tips for managing yourself

1   Take a behavioural audit of your life – assess your current patterns at home and at work and pinpoint the two specific changes which would make the most difference to your personal effectiveness.

2   Cut down on the number of tasks going on at any one time and streamline your workflow by getting rid of excess paperwork, making

▶

lists and creating time-saving routines. Turn your email account off if you need to dedicate yourself to a particular task without distraction.

3   If it suits you better, don't be afraid to work in short, intense bursts, followed by regular breaks and encourage this type of work pattern in your team.

4   Pinpoint your most productive times of day, and assign your most important activities to those times; don't always open your email first thing if this eats up your most valuable time of day.

5   Remember why you do your job to help you get out to work in the morning – identify personal and global objectives, and advance your career by gaining experience which is directly useful to achieving your goals.

6   Try to get a good balance between the four silos of success – happiness, achievement, significance and legacy.

7   Make the most of your inherent personality type – being an introvert is no bad thing if you can impress people with your quiet proficiency.

8   Rationalise your fears by admitting that you don't need to be the best at everything; if public speaking terrifies you (as it does lots of people), remember that the benchmarks are low and mediocrity will usually suffice.

9   Take calculated risks with both your career and your talent; don't be afraid to test yourself with things you might fail at.

10   Be yourself. Nothing loses respect like being a phoney.

Chapter 2
Managing others

What topics are covered in this chapter?

- Spotting and nurturing talent
- Getting the most out of your team
- Managing 'difficult' people
- Fostering peak performance
- Earning respect and trust

> **" "** We don't take people to the elevator – we take them down to the street. **" "**

David Ogilvy

I n its earliest days, before it had discovered the advertising model which would make it billions, Google was an exceedingly frugal company. In 2000, when its first head of sales requested a fax machine, Google's founders, Larry Page and Sergey Brin, demanded to know what it was for, and whether its benefits would outweigh its costs.

And yet, the company managed to attract some of the most brilliant talent around. Computer scientists of the highest calibre were attracted by the idea of working on difficult computing problems with like-minded souls. Great salesmen and managers were ready to give up steady jobs with world-renowned companies to go to work for a shaky company with an unclear future still operating out of a garage in Menlo Park, California. Even when Google had just a few employees it had a culture.

A few years later, once the tills were ringing, Google would lavish perks on its employees. It hired a great San Francisco chef and gave him stock options, which came to be worth millions. Without leaving work, employees could get massages and have their laundry done for them. The offices were designed to increase the interactions and good vibes among employees, to raise the chances of a serendipitous encounter. Page and Brin believed strongly that the key to corporate vibrancy was human density, keeping people close, buzzing and focused on their work.

They also hated golf and refused ever to sponsor a golf event, which was almost unheard for a company so deeply involved in advertising. New salesmen were told that companies which took buyers out on golf outings did so only because they had nothing else to offer. Google would never stoop so low.

Google was resolutely quirky, challenging every managerial orthodoxy with an engineer's scepticism. Why did anything have to be done this way and not that? Disorganisation, the company's leaders bragged, was a feature, a way to ensure that nothing trumped delivering the best experience to the user. Too many companies, Google believed, sacrificed the user experience in favour of meeting internal bureaucratic demands. Customers suffered when divisions warred or trivial procedures hampered innovation. When an engineer wanted to work on a project, he could just go ahead and do it. 'That's the way Google works', one of them said. 'Don't ask for permission for an idea, just go and do it. And then, when you're way beyond the point of no return, you're like, "I need $200 million."'[1]

But as one might imagine, such free-wheeling management gave investors hysterics. The threat of corporate implosion never seemed far away. The challenge became keeping the creativity and innovation while creating a means of monitoring, tracking and measuring objectives and people.

> free-wheeling management gave investors hysterics

Andy Grove, the founder of Intel, the world's biggest maker of electronic chips, used to give a speech about the departure

---

[1] *In the Plex: How Google Thinks, Works, and Shapes our Lives*, Steven Levy, Simone Schuster, 2001, p. 230, quoting Andy Rubin, creator of the Google phone

of Christopher Columbus to the New World. Columbus was in fundamental ways no different from anyone starting a new venture. He had an idea and went out looking for funds. The process took far longer than anticipated. His pitch was that he would find a trade route to the Indies. After years of trying, he finally had his money, so he gathered a crew, bought supplies, crossed the Atlantic and successfully dodged pirates on the way. But rather than finding a route to the East Indies, what he found was the New World of the Americas. Should one consider Columbus a failure, because he had failed in his original mission? Or was it more useful to see how he reached each objective along the way?

Grove believed passionately in a management method called Objectives and Key Results, or OKR, and his adherents included John Doerr, one of the major investors in Google. Doerr pressed Google's founders to try the method out, to see if it helped bridge the chasm between managerial chaos and order. The idea of OKR is that each individual and group has one objective and three measurable key results. You write all of them down and then measure yourself against the key results, rather than the ultimate objective. The idea is to make sure that everyone knows what the organisation is trying to achieve, and then what they as individuals and teams can do to get there. It helps turn the abstraction of a distant goal into a series of concrete steps.

Google being Google went about the measuring piece as only computer scientists could. If you set an objective and met it exactly, you scored 1. If you met only half of your target, you scored 0.5. If you exceeded it by half, you scored 1.5. The ideal score, Google believed, was 0.7, as it suggested you were setting a high standard and coming close to achieving it. If you consistently failed by too much, you were bad at your job. If you always succeeded it suggested you had set unambitious targets for yourself. Ideally, you should have just a few objectives at a time, rather than trying to focus on everything. By keeping your objectives limited in number and precise in detail, you could achieve a balance between managerial oversight and employee empowerment.

Managers at Google were now expected to help set objectives, organise groups, motivate and communicate to them, measure performance and then use those measurements to develop themselves and those they managed.

To the surprise of many inside and outside Google, managing by objectives caught on. The company instituted quarterly and annual OKRs throughout the company and revelled in all the data. It was no longer enough for a project manager to promise that his project would be a success. He would have to say specifically, for example, how many units would be sold by a particular date or how many dollars of advertising revenue sold. Employees started to be measured on their progress towards their OKRs using traffic light colours: green for good, amber for middling and red to show there was a problem. These OKR measures were then posted on every employee's profile on the corporate intranet along with other basic biographical information. It not only helped keep the company on track, but also created an internal culture of competition and aggressive transparency. If everything is in plain sight, then problems can be dealt with quickly and effectively.

To make this kind of monitoring work, though, managers must be accessible and employees must willingly participate. When Google is planning a new product, it 'dogfoods' it, meaning it obliges its employees to 'eat their own dogfood' by using the product prototypes and identifying flaws and making suggestions for improvement. Every Friday, the company still holds TGIF sessions where employees can ask anything they like of Page and Brin.

This transparent, participatory approach also helped in 2008, when Google decided it had to make cuts to employee perks. Rather than managers dictating what had to be cut, they asked their employees. They suggested getting rid of bottled water and the companywide ski-trip.

Managing others, like every aspect of management, is not about adhering to any particular orthodoxy. There is no one-size-fits-all approach, any more than humans are automatons who respond identically to certain stimuli.

Google discovered this and has found ways to manage people in a way consistent with their business objectives. Every manager must do the same.

This chapter includes several ideas for how to think about this, but the best approach can only ever be established in context. And it all begins with finding the right people in the first place.

Hiring for tomorrow

Hiring is the orphan child of management. Far more effort and science goes into budgeting, strategy and operations management than finding the right people. At least in business. All too often, hiring is left to the human resources department, a support function often disparaged by senior executives. In hiring you see the same mistakes made again and again: people are hired for their CVs, rather than who they really are; managers hire others like themselves; people get hired for who they are or who they know, rather than what they can do for you tomorrow.

The basic question to be asked in any hiring process is this: what does my organisation need to get done? Only when you have made a specific list of targets and steps can you even begin to think about who might be the right person to fill the post. Yet all too often, managers focus on qualifications such as degrees or which other companies have hired this person, rather than the right issues, which are what has

> in any hiring process, ask: what does my organisation need to get done?

this person achieved, under what kind of circumstances and leaving what kind of trail behind them. Two people might have achieved identical sales targets in the same industry, but one might have burned through all their relationships in the process while another has been constantly enriching their network.

Even the most accomplished recruiters will tell you that getting to the truth of who people are takes far more effort than most companies invest in it. CEOs and investors say that talent accounts for 50 per cent of all business success, with execution a distant second at 2 per cent, and yet most academic studies of traditional interviewing show that that is not at all predictive of job perform-ance.[2] Most potential hires can scrub up and offer up the right answers to the same old interview questions. It takes multiple rounds and various forms of interrogation to add texture and truth.

Of course, not every position will merit such an investment of effort. But if you are hiring people whom you hope to make responsible and enduring members of your organisation, it is worth jettisoning the usual voodoo habits like trusting your gut and talking about 'corporate fit' and treating hiring with the same diligence you would an acquisition. Create a scorecard for the person you want to hire, then generate a stream of excellent recruits. Candidates who appear excellent on a first pass may fall to pieces on the third or fourth look; others will look better and better.

Managers tend to shy away from mavericks and late bloomers, those who might achieve great things but have unusual pasts. They focus on the past rather than potential. If you can avoid this mistake, it not only expands your pool of talent, but also gives you a route to outsized performance.

Hiring junior staff

When hiring junior staff, the key question to ask is to what degree will your organisation be depending on these people? It is all too easy to think of junior staff as the weakest links in any company.

---

[2] *Who: The A Method for Hiring*, Geoff Smart and Randy Street, Ballantine Books, 2008

But not only do they represent the future, but they can also become highly visible representatives of all that your organisation does. The person sitting at the front desk gives an immediate impression. Whoever takes your phone calls represents you. If you are forced to delegate a lot of analysis and reporting to junior employees, then the quality of your decisions will ultimately depend on the quality of their work.

But then, of course, you must be realistic. The quality of the people you hire will be a direct reflection of the financial and psychological compensation you offer. Money, excitement, interest, good prospects, stability and fun will matter to job applicants in varying measure, and no company will satisfy everyone. But there is no use holding out for that dream candidate when the salary you are offering is poor and the work dreary. In every job interview, the manager may be thinking of meeting a present need, but every candidate is thinking, what would taking this job mean for my future?

Every person you hire will have to satisfy different needs at different levels of compensation. But these needs can be grouped as follows:

1 Basic competence. Do they show up on time? Are they presentable? Are they well organised? Are they honest? This can all be gleaned through references and the first impression.

2 Social profile. Are they warm or frigid? Do they make friends easily, or scare people off? Will they be pleasant to work with? Bring them to lunch with your colleagues and see how they do.

3 Curiosity. Do they have a wide or narrow set of interests beyond work? Are they enthusiastic or reluctant learners? What skill or interest have they acquired in the last five years?

4 Network. Whom do they know professionally and how well? Who have they done business with before who is willing to talk about them?

5 Intellect. Are they brainy? Can they analyse their way through difficult problems? Set them one, perhaps on pencil and paper for half an hour.

6   Tenacity. Do they press on through stressful moments or do they crack? Ask them about the most stressful periods of their life. Honesty and fakery are easy to read in these moments.

7   Creativity. Have they ever taken one of their own ideas and seen it through to completion? Truly creative people own their own ideas, make them happen and will eagerly and quickly be able to describe this process.

It's helpful to keep all these elements in mind when you're recruiting new people to your business; make sure you have a list of questions that address each of these topics during the interview process.

Hiring other managers

Ben Horowitz, a co-founder of Andreessen Horowitz, one of the most successful venture capital firms in Silicon Valley, has three questions he asks when evaluating new CEOs for his companies.

1   Does this CEO know what to do?

Horowitz breaks this up into two separate parts. The first thing an aspiring CEO must understand is strategy, or rather, the company's story. This is more than just a set of goals and objectives. As Horowitz puts it, a story answers a much harder set of questions. 'Why should I join this company? Why should I be excited to work here? Why should I buy your product? Why should I invest in the company? Why is the world better off as a result of this company's existence?'

A great example of executive story-telling was Jeff Bezos's 1997 letter to Amazon shareholders, a succinct three-page summary of what his young company was all about. At the time, Amazon had just 1.5 million customers and less than $150 million in revenue, a fraction of what it would become. But Bezos was brilliantly clear in his vision and purpose. No one investing in or going to work for the company could be in any doubt about Amazon's story.

'Today, online commerce saves customers money and precious time', wrote Bezos. 'Tomorrow, through personalisation, online commerce will accelerate the very process of discovery. Amazon. com uses the Internet to create real value for its customers and, by doing so, hopes to create an enduring franchise, even in established and large markets.'

Bezos emphasised that Amazon was 'all about the long term' and laid out a fundamental management and decision-making approach which he hoped was consistent with his investors' understanding of his company. This approach rested on a relentless focus on customers, on data and analysis, on experimentation and studying failures, on a lean, cost-conscious culture, on hiring excellent employees who felt a sense of ownership in the company, on openness with investors, and on prioritising cash flow over any other accounting measure.

Bezos concluded that he was optimistic but vigilant and urgent about what needed to be done. 'We feel good about what we've done and even more excited about what we want to do', an ideal managerial state of mind.

It is also worth noting that Bezos used three full pages to lay out his story. It would have been trivial expressed as a tagline or simplistic 'vision statement'. One sentence is not enough, ten pages would be too much, but three pages was just right.

The second part of knowing what to do is having the confidence and knowledge to make good and timely decisions. Confidence is what enables a manager to make decisions with incomplete information, and the hardest decisions will inevitably displease someone.

The good CEO or manager must be constantly assembling information to make endless decisions, big and small. There will be little time to crunch through all the information, so decision making often becomes an instinctive act, a good habit based on good practice and a comprehensive view of the problem developed over scores of minute interactions with employees, customers and competitors.

Horowitz's next question is:

2 Can the CEO get the company to do what she wants?

This comes down to a managerial ability to lead through persuading others of your story and then making the kind of sound decisions which can bring it to life. The first part of this will be assembling the right people and giving them sufficient resources. Building a team is a manager's job, not the sole preserve of HR. Excellence is defined by the abilities of a specific group of people to solve a specific problem. Those abilities will be constrained if a company is riddled with infighting and shoddy processes. There is no point hiring a great team and then abandoning them in a bombed-out corporate war zone. They need support and a focused environment in which to get their work done. Building this kind of environment involves sophisticated management of incentives and excellent communication.

3 How do we set results against objectives?

We saw this earlier at Google. Horowitz finds measuring results against objectives valuable, but also sets some useful parameters. Managers, he says, must be measured 'against their company's opportunity – not somebody else's company'.

All too often, managers are told they need to deliver Twitter-like growth, when they are in an industry, solar power, say, which offers nothing like the same cost and scale opportunities. Horowitz tells the story of Robin Li, the CEO of Baidu. When Baidu went public in 2005, its shares nearly quintupled in value on their first day of trading. His investors and employees were delighted, yet Li was miserable. He told Horowitz that he was all set to deliver results appropriate to a price per share of $27, and now he would have to deliver results befitting a share price of $122. He felt obliged to produce results which matched the market's expectations. He focused on his company's operations, technology and users, and delivered. But how many managers would have felt the same sense of duty to a share price?

More important is to figure out your opportunity and what you want to do, and decide on who needs to achieve what intermediate results to get you there.

Jagged résumés, talent that whispers and talent that shouts

George Anders coined these three terms in his book *The Rare Find*. They describe the kind of talent hirers should be looking for, but rarely do. The 'jagged résumé' belongs to a job applicant who has taken some risks and followed a less orthodox path through life. They may have dropped out of university, or been through a few jobs. They might have taken a year or two to live somewhere far away or gone on an unusual adventure. But for the discerning recruiter, these résumés offer greater insight into an applicant's character than a thousand other superficially more impressive CVs. The companies which took the time to understand these unusual applicants tended to have figured out in their own minds what were trainable skills and what were the character traits which would lead to long-term success. A candidate may never have built a spreadsheet or presented in PowerPoint, but if they can demonstrate a great work ethic, intelligence and a dedication to doing what they say they will, they could make a far better hire than someone with a few commoditised office skills. The US Special Forces tests candidates in gruelling endurance tests. But it is not just looking for the fittest or strongest candidates. It wants candidates with cunning and resilience, problem-solvers who quickly bounce back from adversity. Fitness can be acquired. Resilience, after a certain age, cannot.

Talent that whispers similarly tends to lie beyond the mainstream recruiting channels. When Facebook started, it badly needed

> talent that whispers tends to lie beyond the mainstream recruiting channels

programmers. As a start-up it could not pay the top salaries found at Microsoft or Google. It needed to find talent outside the closed world of Silicon Valley. So in 2006 it used its own website to set programming puzzles and invited anyone to try to solve them.

'We developed this theory that occasionally there were these brilliant people out there who hadn't found their way to Silicon Valley', said Yishan Wong, the engineer given the job of setting the puzzles. 'They might be languishing in ordinary tech jobs. We needed a way to surface them.'[3] Within months, Facebook was deluged with these 'geniuses from nowhere', emerging from the hordes of programmers all over the world who took up the company's puzzle challenge. By 2011, the puzzle process had led to the hiring of 118 engineers, nearly 20 per cent of Facebook's crack programmers.

Talent that shouts is made up of that difficult bunch whose talent is undisputed, but whose ambitions and potential for frustration and petulance are limitless. These people need to be reminded constantly that talent is never enough, unless harnessed to hard work and collegiality. They also need to be challenged rather than coddled. They appreciate pitting their skills against the very hardest problems and being put in extreme situations. There is a good chance they will flame out, but there is an equal chance they will succeed on a dramatic scale. Managers cannot shy away from such talent. Instead they must find a way to harness it so it is not destructive to the organisation, then give it freedom and endless challenges. They must imagine above all what can go right by hiring such talent, rather than fretting over what might go wrong.

---

[3] *The Rare Find: Spotting Brilliance before Anyone Else*, George Anders, Viking, 2011, p. 122

Case Study

Reed Hastings, who founded the online movie rental company Netflix, uses the term 'talent density' to describe his hiring policy. Behind it is the idea that the very best people are not just a little bit better than the rest, but as much as five times better. When hiring then, if you can identify and recruit the best, you won't just be a nose ahead of your competitors but way out in front. By hiring fewer, more talented people, Hastings believes he can avoid the dreaded 'big-company creep'. Fewer people means less office politics and less bureaucracy. Fewer people with meddlesome 'cc' emails. But it also means much more is expected of those who are hired. They are expected to do the work of three or four mere mortals.

In return, they are exceptionally well compensated and given unlimited holiday. Netflix recruiters are told that when it comes to attracting talent, money is no object. The idea is that responsible employees will do what is asked of them and not take advantage of the company. In return for excellent pay and extraordinary freedom, they will be expected to do great things. Pay is not linked to performance reviews or a bonus pool. Employees can decide whether they want to be paid in cash or stock, and there is no vesting schedule on their options. Netflix does not believe in handcuffing employees to the company with options. Instead, it trusts that its open, free culture will attract and keep the very best working and innovating there rather than anywhere else.

Getting past stereotypes and charisma

The most common problem in hiring is stereotyping. The moment someone enters an office, he or she is judged, before they have made their opening moves or had a chance to discuss their CV. Managers frequently hire people who look and sound just like themselves and in the process miss out on the people who could do great things for their organisation.

This bias exists at every level of business. CEOs, for example, tend to be a shade taller than average men. A poll of Fortune 500 CEOs in America taken by the writer Malcolm Gladwell found that around 30 per cent of them were 6'2" or taller, versus just 3.9 per cent of all adult men.[4] Of the tens of millions of American men 5'6" or smaller, just ten had made it into the top CEO ranks, suggesting it is just as hard or even harder for a short man to break into the top ranks of American business as it is for a woman or African-American male.

It seems we all have a sense of what a CEO should look like, and those who fit the profile; tall, confident, white, males rise more quickly and frequently through the corporate ranks. Several studies have shown that taller men earn more than their shorter counterparts, several hundred pounds per inch. An Australian study concluded that in salary terms, an extra two inches in height equated to an extra year in working experience.[5] Compounded over a working life, it means that taller managers on average make hundreds of thousands of pounds more than shorter ones, without being any better at what they do.

As a manager, you will be wasting your money, as well as being victim to your silent prejudices, if you fail to recognise patterns like these. So much hiring, even at the highest levels, is based on irrational perceptions of people's worth. Most companies over-pay and over-promote people for the wrong reasons, creating a cost and hiring advantage for managers able to see through and act at odds with the most popular prejudices.

> so much hiring is based on irrational perceptions of people's worth

---

[4] *Blink: The Power of Thinking without Thinking*, Malcolm Gladwell, Penguin, 2006
[5] 'Does Size Matter in Australia?', Michael Kortt and Andrew Leigh, *The Economic Record*, Vol. 86, No. 272, March 2010, pp. 71–83

We can see evidence of this on the covers of many business magazines: the CEO as hero, arms folded, staring out purposefully into the future. If the editors of these titles are right, we admire CEOs who radiate the confidence of a newly elected politician or a movie star launching a Christmas blockbuster. We like our CEOs to come from central casting. We venerate those who breathe new life into dying organisations, who execute dramatic turnarounds or mergers, who launch world-changing new products. We seem to covet the theatrical in managers, even when that is the last thing most good management is about.

Our tendency to overestimate the effect of an individual in any situation is referred to by sociologists as the 'fundamental attribution error'. We venerate the heroic figure over teams or processes, and this is as common in business as it is in warfare, politics or the arts.

And yet, as Rakesh Khurana of the Harvard Business School has written:

> *What makes today's profound faith in the charismatic CEO so troubling is the lack of any conclusive evidence linking leadership to organizational performance. In fact, most academic research that has sought to measure the impact of CEOs confirms Warren Buffett's observation that when you bring good management into a bad business, it's the reputation of the business that stays intact. Studies show that various internal and external constraints inhibit an executive's ability to affect a company's performance. Most estimates, for example, attribute anywhere from 30 per cent to 45 per cent of performance to industry effects and 10 per cent to 20 per cent to year-to-year economic changes. Thus, the best anyone can say about the effect of a CEO on a company's performance is that it depends greatly on circumstances.* [6]

---

[6] 'The Curse of the Superstar CEO', Rakesh Khurana, *Harvard Business Review*, September 2002

Yet time and again, we see organisations trumpeting the brilliant individual over the brilliant team. When a problem needs to be solved, companies often look outside for answers. They see their own people as part of the problem, and seek external managers who can come in with fresh ideas and no internal, political baggage. Tough work is seen to require tough outsiders, capable of slashing and burning without emotion. This view works unfairly to the detriment of hard-working insiders who given the chance might be just as good at bringing about change.

It also leads to dangerous organisational habits, such as excessive faith in charisma over reason. Jeff Skilling, the CEO who led Enron into the abyss, cast himself as a bold, innovative thinker, a man who engaged in daredevil physical pursuits at the weekend and led his company into new markets during the week. But ultimately, he was what he was. An MBA and management consultant running on a dangerous adrenaline high. His managers dared not challenge his crazier ideas for fear of seeming unimaginative or old-school. His CFO, who was ultimately jailed for cooking Enron's books, was so taken by Skilling he named one of his children after him. Skilling developed devotees rather than good managers, to the extent that no one was willing to tell him that he was running his company, and the fate of thousands of employees and shareholders, off a cliff.

Taking the time to develop an accurate view of people's talents and capabilities, and not letting yourself be over-impressed by the new, is vital in the hiring and managing of others. Starting by breaking our mental link between height and competence is just the start.

Managing teams

Managing individuals and managing teams are separate challenges. When a manager arrives in a new job, he will almost always take care to get to know the individual members of his team. He will learn their names, their abilities, their hopes and insecurities. He may take them out for lunch one by one, or invite them in for individual meetings. But it will take longer to understand how they work together as a team. No one can force a group of people to work amicably and effectively together. Successful teamwork happens when people choose to work as a team. They must want to work for you, for each other or for the goals you set them. Creating an environment for successful teamwork and collaboration is quite different from managing people one by one.

> successful teamwork happens when people choose to work as a team

And yet consider some of the obstacles to achieving this. Go back to the 1950s and 1960s, when companies were much more hierarchical and geographically narrow, and the work of managers tended to be much more limited. Managers mostly worked in a specific function, such as manufacturing or accounting, handling a single market. They knew that provided they kept showing up for work, their loyalty would be rewarded with a job for life. Their colleagues were colleagues for 30 years. Work started at 9 am and ended at 5 pm, Monday to Friday. Weekends were their own and travel was only for the most senior in an organisation.

Compare that to the 21st century, when work never seems to end. When teams operate across oceans and time zones. When customers have abundant choices and force those who serve them to come back with new offerings overnight, when your competitors can take advantage of dramatically lower labour costs, when every manager is expected to grasp and integrate every business function and bundle them into a customer solution – all in the knowledge that the ideas of job security and companies being loyal to employees have gone the way of typing pools and the three- Martini lunch.

Companies need teams to work more effectively than ever, but what's in it for their workers?

An effective team is one whose output meets or exceeds what is expected of it. This might be creating a product, a profit or simply coming up with an idea. It must also provide a sense of fulfilment for its members. This does not require that it always be enjoyable. Rather that it serves as a vehicle for meaningful and improving work for each of its members, some of which may be hard and repetitive, but is ultimately satisfying. If it does this, then the team will achieve enduring success as its members will want to work together and learn together with ever more impressive results. Managers will fail if they focus solely on output and neglect the subtler processes of team learning and purposeful work. A fractious but lucky team may win once. But a team focused on enhancing each member's performance and shared improvement will keep winning and coming close year after year, luck be damned.

The work of managing teams can be broken into two parts. The first is managing externally. For a team to function effectively it needs to know where it stands, who its competitors are, what its purpose within and without the organisation is, what resources it has at its disposal and what support it has. No team can work well for long if its work is constantly undermined from outside, or underfunded or misdirected. It is the job of the manager to maintain external relations, to harvest the necessary resources from outside and erect the necessary protections so that the team can get on with its work.

The second part is managing internally. It may sound obvious, but many people may not even realise that they are part of a team. They understand they work for an organisation, or even for a group within an organisation. But it does not necessarily follow that they see their work as dependent on that of others. Many organisations set up workflows so that individuals can punch in and out of work with no sense of the relevance of their role within a team. They are led to believe that as long as they do their narrowly defined job, they are making a contribution. So the first task for the manager may just be to gather the team so that it understands that it possesses a collective identity.

The next task is to establish the work of a team. In some cases an output may have already been determined, in others it may be more vague. The manager must then decide to what extent he wishes to involve the team in laying out a plan to achieve its goal. In a team where each member has highly specialised skills, the manager's primary role will be that of integrator, deferring to each expert, but enabling these varied talents to work effectively together. In a team where skills and confidence are low, the manager may need to be more directive, laying out a clear path to victory, hoping that over time his team members will be able to participate more and more in finding solutions and success.

It is fashionable to talk of the need to secure employee 'buy-in' to management, but there is no off-the-rack solution to securing this. Where employees are seasoned and expert, they will expect to be heard and involved in any decision making. Where they are naive and new to the work, they may prefer to be given clear direction.

The very word 'team' is not as generic as we might like. Even within sports, we see very different models.[7] When a country sends its 'team' to the Olympics, it is sending a group of people who excel in their individual disciplines but whose interaction is extremely limited. At the end of the games, their achievements may be measured collectively in the number of medals their nation has won, but a gymnast has nothing to do with a pentathlete, or a sailor with a sprinter. Each nation's Olympic committee may have worked for years to create the structures and provide the support which enables these athletes to succeed. But each individual athlete trains, improves and succeeds according to his own talents and efforts. They can afford to be hugely selfish in how they go about achieving their goals.

Compare this with a soccer team, where each player has highly developed specialist skills related to the position they play. The

---

[7] 'There's More than One Kind of Team', Peter Drucker, *Wall Street Journal*, 11 February 1992

goalkeeper has fast reflexes to block shots, the striker is fast and opportunistic, while the defender may be much more strategic and physical in how he plays. They may all have basic levels of athleticism, but their talents have evolved in very different ways. As you watch them play, their individual gifts are on display, but so too is their ability to play in a team, which is all that is measured in the eventual score. A selfish but talented player will quickly lose the trust of his team-mates, while a shrinking violet may lack the resolve to take control of a failing situation. Soccer requires talented individuals who know how to blend their individual, specific talents into the work of a team.

A third model, and one which is most coveted these days, is that of the tennis doubles team. This is a self-managed team in which each player is interchangeable and capable of filling in and doing the work of the other. You cannot deflect responsibility by passing the ball to a team-mate. If it comes whizzing at you, you are expected to play your shot. In a traditional hierarchical model, it was much easier to defer, to slink away from responsibility. In this tennis doubles model, each team member is much more exposed. For those willing and able to commit, trust and collaborate, this can be enormously empowering and exciting. For those less confident about their work or unconvinced by the benefits of such teamwork, it can seem frightening and unfair.

When selecting a team, a manager must seek to achieve a balance between collaboration and conflict. If all he wants is a team that gets along, then he might select people who are very like each other and who communicate easily. But if he wants a team which finds novel, creative solutions to problems, he must accept different personalities, perspectives and talents. He must accept the inevitability of misunderstandings and disputes as his team works towards its goal. But

> some degree of conflict is the price of doing difficult and meaningful work

some degree of conflict is the price of doing difficult and ultimately meaningful work. If all you do is glide along well-oiled and familiar tracks, competitors will soon overtake you. Set up too much conflict within a team, however, and you may find it equally ineffective.

The manager must weigh up the importance of adding product, market or functional expertise to a team, with the personalities that expertise comes with. If a team relies heavily on friendship and trust to work well, then an untrustworthy, unlikeable addition, however talented, could be toxic. Similarly, if the relationships within the team are more professional than personal, more clinical and objective, then personality may be much less relevant.

The ultimate measurements of the team's success, however, will be whether it achieves what it sets out to do, and whether its members learn from or desire to repeat the experience. If a team meets its target, but its members find no measure of fulfilment in the process, then its manager will have failed as surely as if he made everyone happy but failed to produce the desired output.

In an ideal situation, influence in a team is accorded in line with expertise. If you are the team member with deep knowledge of finance, you are listened to when it comes to financial issues. The same with design or marketing. The experts hold sway in their respective fields. But rarely does this pan out. Influence tends to follow more random paths. Some people wield it by dint of their personalities or their experience. Some people may talk a lot, while others may have powerful relationships with senior managers beyond the team. It is up to the manager to recognise and moderate these various forms of influence in order to establish the process and habits of the team. The greatest poison in any team is a sense of unfairness. If anyone feels ignored, or unfairly treated, it will quickly lead to resentment which leads to poor performance.

So it is vital that a manager establishes the right habits early and reinforces them often. He can only do this after taking note of the personalities and talents of the team. No manager can enforce 'norms' on a team, but he can introduce processes and discipline which stimulate or limit certain behaviours. If team members are new to each other, for example, frequent and well-directed meetings may be helpful. If they have well-established and successful working habits, then the new manager may be best standing back. If an individual team member appears to be holding back, then it is the manager's job to pull them into discussions. Some teams may respond well to organised team-building exercises, others may never forgive you for them. A well-run team will have mechanisms in place for analysing its own performance and self-correcting, but if it doesn't, a manager must introduce a way to provide constructive and collaborative feedback. Feedback which is clumsily delivered, in a way that shows a lack of awareness of the team's work and challenges, or personal insensitivity, can be even more destructive than no feedback at all. But again, the most important thing is to act early and often. Habits, once entrenched, become very hard to change.

When attempting to improve a team's process, the manager must be very clear about where any problems lie. Is it a question of lack of effort? Or lack of skill? A problem with the strategic approach? Or does the problem lie outside the team, with the larger organisation, or even the market? Extreme clarity around these issues will allow the manager to be properly understood and the team to make the correct adjustments. The more specific you can be about a problem and how it might be addressed, the more willing you will find team members to participate in a process of constant improvement. Blanket criticism is a sure way to seed destructive resentments.

There are essentially four sets of clashing forces inherent to managing teams:

● *The individual versus the team.* Not everyone wants to be part of a team, and not all talents are easily subsumed into a team effort. And yet, no individual is capable of all a team can achieve. There are inefficiencies to teamwork. An individual does not have to hold meetings with himself, give himself progress updates or politic against himself. But with these inefficiencies can come enormous advantages of shared knowledge and effort.

- *Collaboration versus confrontation.* Conflict is uncomfortable, but it is also inevitable when new ideas are being shaped, formed and implemented. You want your team to get along, but you also want them challenged and goaded, to be exposed to new ideas and realities and pressured to perform to a higher level. How do you balance team harmony with the clash of ideas vital to progress?

- *Performance versus development.* The relentless demands of performance often leave no time to reflect, learn and improve. But it is vital to step off the hamster wheel now and again and invest time and effort in learning and improving. It is similar to a racing driver coming into the pits, to change tyres and refuel, briefly losing time against his rivals but knowing that he will ultimately be rewarded as he comes out faster than before. By giving a team time to learn and develop, a manager is also enabling the sense of personal fulfilment in a way that performance alone cannot.

- *Managerial authority versus team autonomy.* Any manager wants his team to feel empowered and happy and to collaborate without constant monitoring. But there will inevitably be goals and deadlines to be met, and teams will often look to managers to set in place the habits and processes which will lead to the achievement of these goals in a way that is satisfying to each team member. The manager must be both a team player and apart from the team, retaining enough of his own authority and influence to manage and lead when issues arise inside and outside the team.

Based on these inevitable clashes, a popular way to think about managing teams is through a triangle of relationships.[8]

---

[8] *Managing in the New Team Environment: Skills, Tools, and Methods*, Larry Hirschhorn, iUniverse, 1991

If a manager pays too much attention to individuals, they may tend to think they have special relationships with the manager, and this creates conflicts of authority and mistrust. The manager quickly loses faith in the notion of the group ever working together as a team. Similarly, if the manager pays too much attention to the team, individuals may feel neglected and pull back. This can engender passivity and a similar collapse in the manager's authority and hopes.

It is useful, then, to imagine managing teams as a dynamic process in which you never wish to be too close to any point on the triangle, but constantly on the move adjusting your levels of attention and direct influence to maximise the talents, the sense of involvement and the willingness to work hard and collaborate which will eventually determine your team's success.

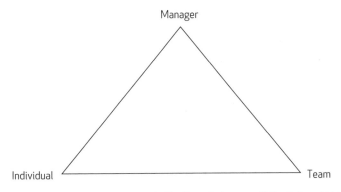

Source: Hirschhorn, Larry, *Managing in the New Team Environment: Skills, Tools, and Methods* San Jose, CA: Authors Choice Press © 2002. Reprinted with permission.

Managing clever people

Every successful CEO will tell you that it is vital to surround yourself with people cleverer than yourself. They will fill in the gaps in your own talents as well as come up with great ideas and give you useful feedback. But this comes with its own challenges.

As a manager of an industrial process, you may be able to hide who you are. If you are managing a creative or intellectual process you will be examined top to bottom by your staff. Every one of your qualities and failings will be picked apart by people who prize themselves on their judgement of others.

> by far the safest course of action is to be yourself

In such a setting, by far the safest course of action is to be yourself. To be anything else risks eventual exposure and humiliation.

Most employees want to have the best brought out of them. They see the company as a means to personal fulfilment. But this is no starry-eyed vision. They also see it as a means to financial survival. A good manager understands both and shows loyalty to his reports as much as to his bosses. By showing loyalty to those you manage you reduce the cynicism which can bedevil so much work in organisations. A single demonstration of loyalty by a manager to an employee is worth a thousand regurgitations of the corporate culture document.

In a company of smart people, you are bound to have differences of opinion. No matter how well you set up a discussion, people will always disagree. The smarter your employees, the greater the disagreement. The best way to handle this is by having an utterly transparent process. One in which each step of the decision making is explained. Then if people disagree, at least they will know how a decision is reached and feel that they received at least a fair hearing. It is better to be impartial and fair than nice.

When management theorists talk of the 'span' and 'scope' of management tasks, they are talking about distance. Are you so far above your employees you pale into irrelevance? Or so close to a few that you cannot control the many? A manager who gathers so much power that scores of people are waiting on his every word is likely to be extremely inefficient. Likewise, what's the point of having a manager for a small group who can easily get along without one?

Clans are useful in creating team spirit. But they also lead to closed-mindedness. You need to break them up every now and again to invigorate them. You need to go outside your own group and find knowledge across the organisation.

Using perverse incentives[9]

Our lives are entirely composed of incentives, from the promise of breakfast in the morning and the fears and rewards around attending school or work, to the anticipation of a hot bath at night. All of our behaviours are stimulated by various incentives. They can be short- or long-term, a pay rise next quarter, or the hope that one day you might be CEO. Incentives can be positive or negative, carrots or sticks. Their existence is a fact. How you manage them is up to you. Depending on your orchestration of the incentive system, you will elicit either desirable or undesirable behaviour from your employees.

Psychologists and economists are collaborating as never before to expand the field of behavioural economics, to tell us why we behave the way we do when it comes to work and money. So why are companies so slow to rethink how they manage their people? Why are they so much more innovative when it comes to jiggering with their balance sheet or product line than human resources?

Dan Ariely, a professor of behavioural economics at Duke University and author of the books *Predictably Irrational* and *The Upside of Irrationality*, says that while companies harry him for insights into customer behaviour, they are often loath to try out anything new on their employees. 'There is no worse place to try to do experiments than Human Resources. The first thing on their mind when they hear the word "experiment" is lawsuits.'

---

[9] Parts of this section are taken from Delves Broughton, P., 'Break the model on employee behaviour', *The Financial Times*, October 2010. © The Financial Times Limited 2010. All rights reserved. For the full article, see the appendix at the back of the book.

This is a great shame and offers an opportunity for managers bold enough to test out something new. For example, Prof. Ariely has found from researching bankers' bonuses that they have next to no impact on performance. Banks, he argues, would be better off firing all but their most talented employees and hiring thousands of new workers with none of the salary and bonus expectations of the old ones. They would be able to do the same work for much less money, unburdened by outlandish expectations. It is part of his broader case that we are all spurred on or inhibited by a complex web of motivations which affect each of us differently. These include a sense of purpose, status, altruism, ego and control, all of which a clever manager should take into account. And yet how many do this in anything but the most informal way?

No company enjoys bonus season. Productivity falls as people hover around waiting to hear what they are getting each year. But once a system like this is well entrenched, it is very hard to change. The easiest time for a company to get its incentives right is when it is still young and growing.

Prof. Ariely says he receives plenty of calls from start-ups, brimming with enthusiasm for new organisational forms. They crave new ideas about compensation and how to improve employee morale and creativity. They are eager to use unconventional methods to motivate individuals who spend their days working away from the main office on unusual schedules, and may only ever see parts rather than the whole of a business.

But once these companies reach any kind of scale, the experimental mindset hardens into a procedural one. The enthusiasm to get the most out of every individual becomes a desire to settle on a one-size-fits-all motivational template, regardless of the irrational behaviours it might cause.

The only way Prof. Ariely has found through this inertia is to get the chief executive onside. He began working with Scott Cook of Intuit, the financial software company, on experiments to understand the behaviour of his customers. Why, for example, do people pay off their smallest loans before those that carry the highest interest rates? He suggested creating a software tool to help customers behave more rationally. From small beginnings, this behavioural economics research seeped into Intuit's internal organisation. Instead of offering purely financial incentives for great work, Intuit now offers high-performing employees half a year's sabbatical. At Prof. Ariely's urging, Cook encouraged a more supportive culture of experimentation, telling employees that a failed experiment is no failure if it produces evidence. This is vital to employees' feelings of control.

Innovative management that takes the complexity of human behaviour into account can be a competitive advantage – especially now, when so few are ready to practise it.

Motivating people

Professors Edward Deci and Richard Ryan at the University of Rochester and Mihaly Csikszentmihalyi at Claremont Graduate University have found that we do our best work when motivated from within, when we have control over our time and decisions and when we feel a deep sense of purpose. Under such conditions, we can achieve real mastery over whatever it is that we do.

The modern workplace, however, is too often set up to deny us this opportunity. Firms that hope to optimise efficiency by making their employees clock in and out, attend compulsory meetings, and receive pay for performance are de-motivating through excessive control. What they should be doing, according to modern motivation theory, is giving workers the chance to do their best work by granting them more autonomy and helping them to achieve the mastery that may come with it.

If pay and promotions were all that mattered, why would anyone labour to write Wikipedia entries? Or do volunteer work? Some firms like Google and 3M have taken advantage of their vast revenues to allow their employees to spend 20 per cent of their time on personal projects. This policy has yielded Google News and the Post-it Note. Best Buy, the electronics retailer, has experimented with a 'results oriented work environment' at its corporate headquarters in Minnesota, in a bid to raise morale and lower turnover. Salaried employees are told to do their jobs on their own schedule. If they need to duck out to a doctor's appointment with their child, they don't need to ask. It is assumed they will get their work done in their own time. The hope is that, in such an environment, workers will feel more inclined to contribute to the company's well-being than they would if they were simply grinding out hours for a pay cheque.

These are old lessons made new. Beyond serving our basic needs, money doesn't buy happiness. We need a greater purpose in our lives. Our most precious resource is time. We respond badly to conditions of servitude, whether the lash of the galley master or the more subtle enslavement of monthly pay cheques, quarterly performance targets and the fear of losing health insurance. Work that allows us to feel in control of our lives is better than work that does not. However hoary these messages, managers would do well to recall them and do their best to recognise these principles in how they treat others.

An underestimated but invaluable management habit is simply to be nice. Managers who bother to treat people as people rather than economic instruments have a natural advantage. In their landmark management book *In Search of Excellence*, the American consultants Tom Peters and Bob Waterman, coined the phrase 'hard is soft, soft is hard'. After studying dozens of American corporations in the early 1980s, they found that all that was considered 'hard' in business, the numbers and plans, were soft and easily manipulable, while the 'soft' subjects ignored by business schools, such as character, and dealing with people inside and outside the organisation, were hard and vitally important.

Since then, Peters has gone even further, repeating novelist Henry James's claim that 'three things in human life are important: the first is to be kind. The second is to be kind. And the third is to be kind.' True to his roots as an engineer, Peters even formulated an equation: $K = R = P$ (Kindness = Repeat Business = Profit). Managers should not fear being nice, for fear of mixing business with pleasure, or feeling inhibited if they then have to make hard decisions. The moment you set up a business and hire someone or sell to a customer, business becomes personal. And once it's personal, it pays to be nice.

Keeping it simple

Based in Chicago, 37signals is a small company with an outsized punch. Mid-2010, it employed just 16 people in three countries to build online web tools; by April 2011, it had 26 employees. Thanks to its software and a talkative founder, it had developed a disproportionate influence among those attempting to change the way we work.

Technology has been promising for years to liberate us from traditional working habits. And while there may be more people working from coffee shops these days, many technology solutions have become added burdens. Wireless communication made us far more mobile but it also made us permanently available.

The business of 37signals is in taking the disorganised spaghetti of emails, documents, calendars, contact lists and to-do lists and creating something usable. It makes just six products, which are used by three million customers to talk, communicate and organise online. It also has a unique management philosophy, tailored to its employees and its time. At the heart of this philosophy is the belief that business is often made far too complicated. When businesses should be small, nimble and independent-minded, instead they grow and become hostage to HR departments and policy meetings which generate neither new products nor new sales.

This complexity is reflected in companies' products and services which become as dense and over-wrought as the organisations which create them. Smaller firms, 37signals believes, can embrace the constraints of their size to create simpler, cleaner products.

Workaholism, for example, 37signals argues, is a symptom of large companies. Workaholics try to make up for intellectual laziness by brute force, hanging around the office, making unreasonable demands, and trying to fix problems by throwing hours at them, rather than pausing to find an intelligent, creative solution. They mistake time spent at the office for actual care over their work.

> workaholics mistake time spent at the office for actual care over their work

Similarly meetings often do nothing but suck the productivity out of an organisation. At 37signals, they set a timer at the start of each meeting and finish when it rings. They recommend inviting as few people as possible, beginning each meeting with a specific problem which must be solved, and ending the meeting with a solution and someone responsible for implementing it.

They call long-term business planning 'fantasy' and say it would be more honest to call the process 'guessing' rather than planning. Calling 'planning' 'guessing' would take the stress out of it. On the other hand, marketing should not be confined to the marketing department but considered part of everything a company does, from the quality of its product to the attitude of its employees. A better term for it would be 'getting the word out'.

For a certain kind of manager, the way 37signals goes about managing might seem anathema. But it is enormously popular among young technology workers. In fact more and more of them expect this kind of workplace, where productivity and effectiveness are prized over presence or politics. If you want to hire the best young people today, it is well worth staying abreast of what they want from work, given the choices they now have to work for others or for themselves.

Handling crisis junkies[10]

Ambitious managers love a crisis. It gives them a chance to shine, to deploy all those talents that may lead to greatness. Former US President Bill Clinton has spoken regretfully that no epic challenges occurred while he was President. Negotiating the North American Free Trade Agreement and implementing limited welfare reform will not get him carved on to Mount Rushmore. It is the same in business. Every chief executive and manager would like to make elephants dance, the way Lou Gerstner did at IBM or turn round an industrial dinosaur as Sergio Marchionne did at Fiat. No one wants to leave a legacy of average performance in dull times.

But there are true crises and manufactured ones – the real-life 'burning platform' that leads to change, and the manager who likes to run amok with his hair on fire so that he feels important or because he cannot get people to do what he wants in a less hyster-ical way. Such people thrive on deadlines and pressure, on price twitches and deal schedules. Creating a permanent sense of siege and looming disaster unless a contract is signed or a trade executed is part of the culture of certain industries, like investment banking.

But standing up to crisis junkies and distinguishing between the various phases of a crisis is an essential managerial skill. Ronald Heifetz, a leadership expert at Harvard's Kennedy School of Government, has defined two phases in crisis management: the emergency, when your priority is to stabilise the situation and buy time; and the adaptive phase, when you address the underlying causes of the crisis in order to build the strength to thrive anew.

---

[10] Parts of this section are taken from Delves Broughton, P., 'Time to stand up to the crisis junkies', *The Financial Times*, 5 September 2011. © The Financial Times Limited 2011. All rights reserved. For the full article, see the appendix at the back of the book.

Great managers understand the difference. In the emergency phase, managers are expected to respond with certainty, to draw on their experience in order to calm nerves. In the second phase, however, they must be extremely open to change. They must be able to set aside their experience, the default behaviours that enabled them to stabilise the emergency, and draw on new ideas in order to adapt their organisations. It is rare to find managers who can do both.

We see variations on this theme throughout business. Turnaround specialists exist purely to come into troubled organisations and fix them, arriving and leaving with no emotional baggage. Start-up entrepreneurs are often replaced by investors as their businesses reach a steady state of growth. The energy and reflexes required for months of high intensity are ill-suited to years of assiduous grunt work. Yet few managers who have led a company well through a crisis will be happy to stand aside for the adaptive phase.

In a 2009 book[11] written with Alexander Grashow and Marty Linsky, Prof. Heifetz wrote: 'Many people survive heart attacks, but most cardiac surgery patients soon resume their old ways: only about 20 per cent give up smoking, change their diet, or get more exercise. In fact, by reducing the sense of urgency, the very success of the initial treatment creates the illusion of a return to normalcy. The medical experts' technical prowess, which solves the immediate problem of survival, inadvertently lets patients off the hook.' If they walk out of the operating room and return to life as before, without, as Heifetz puts it, hitting the 'organizational reset button', they will have wasted a great opportunity, choosing to prolong the emergency rather than do the hard work of adaptation.

Another crucial part of the adaptive phase of crisis management is introducing a 'war game' scenario planning mentality so that

---

[11] *The Practice of Adaptive Leadership: Tools and Tactics for Changing your Organization and the World*, R.A. Heifetz, M. Linsky and A. Grashow, Harvard Business School Press, 2009

you and your organisation become ready to take on the next great emergency. Crises may provide a rush of adrenaline, but if they keep coming they will soon overwhelm you. It is better to adapt to minimise the minor crises, so that when a real one comes along you are fully charged and ready to fight through it.

> it is better to adapt to minimise the minor crises

Learning from hedge funds[12]

Saying you admire hedge funds, beyond some very narrow circles, makes you immediately unpopular. What's to like about those economic vandals, smashing and grabbing their way to billions while the rest of the world wades through the treacle of post-crisis recovery?

But for all the venom directed their way, it is worth considering how these vital players in our economic life are managed. Is there some management system beyond good asset selection, nimble trading and an eye-watering compensation system that makes hedge funds go?

Ray Dalio, founder of Bridgewater, a $90bn fund managed by 1000 employees, is one of a few hedge fund titans to have written a theory of management. Called 'Principles' it reads like a curious mating of Ayn Rand and the Dalai Lama, with a dash of sharp-elbowed MBA. Mr Dalio's company is 35 years old but he founded it just two years out of business school. The key theme of Principles is the importance of truth, 'radical truth' and 'radical transparency', in an organisation designed to foster and profit from original investment ideas. There must be truth around analysis, character, trust and, of course, compensation.

---

[12] Parts of this section are taken from Delves Broughton, P., 'Hedge fund lessons on letting stars shine', *The Financial Times*, 25 April 2011. © The Financial Times Limited 2011. All rights reserved. For the full article, see the appendix at the back of the book.

As Mr Dalio writes, 'pursuing self-interest in harmony with the laws of the universe and contributing to evolution is universally rewarded', even when that pursuit involves operating 'like a hyena attacking the wildebeest'. *More Money than God*, Sebastian Mallaby's history of hedge funds, contains stories of management lunacy that make Mr Dalio's jungle metaphors seem tame. Michael Steinhardt, one of the greatest traders of the 1970s and 1980s, realised his temper was creating dysfunction within his company, so he allowed a psychiatrist to talk to his employees. The psychiatrist kept hearing phrases such as 'battered children', 'random violence' and 'rage disorder'. Mr Steinhardt eventually lost his temper with the shrink and threw him out. Julian Robertson, founder of Tiger Management, one of the most successful hedge funds of the 1980s and 1990s, would try to bond analysts by leading them on macho adventures into the mountains.

Hedge funds are managed more like old-school Hollywood studios than financial institutions. They exist to support one or perhaps a handful of supposed investment geniuses – the talent. When the people who manage them are also the ones making the nerve-jangling investment decisions, it makes for a combustible atmosphere. Financial incentives, which can be colossal, tend to govern everything. Performance is measured in fractions of a basis point rather than 360-degree review sessions. Talent is rewarded lavishly and failure punished swiftly.

Lynn Stratton, a law professor at UCLA, has written that hedge funds are 'criminogenic' environments. She argues that hedge fund managers give the impression that all that matters is maximising returns, ethics be damned, and that financial crimes are victimless. Well, some of them maybe. But they stand at the end of a long line of far better-known companies that have wreaked more damage with similar cultures. Subprime mortgage lenders and those who recklessly securitised bad loans spring to mind.

Aside from enriching their best managers, hedge funds have earned billions for pension plans and endowments over the years, providing diversification where more ordinary financial institutions could not. The best have proved enduring, profitable, stable and innovative. Their most important management feature is the ability to manage billions of dollars with just a few people. No hedge fund manager sets out to build the next JPMorgan Chase or Fidelity. In 2011, Paulson & Co., run by John Paulson, employed 115 people to manage about $35bn in assets, or $304m per employee. Fidelity, the mutual fund and financial services group, by contrast, managed $3500bn with 37,000 employees, or $94m per employee. Mr Paulson is liberated by the size of his organisation to do what he does best – punt on the collapse of the housing market or the rise in the price of gold.

Another vital piece of hedge fund management is requiring employees to keep their money in the company. About 40 per cent of Paulson & Co.'s assets under management belong to the partners and employees. Any investor knows the managers have a stake in the game.

Hedge funds also tend to pay their support staff well. Receptionists, secretaries and chefs are handsomely rewarded for making the lives of the investors and analysts easier. It cuts to the central management challenge of managing the talent, these difficult, gifted people who generate outsized returns. You do that by creating an environment for them to focus on what it is they do extraordinarily well. Bureaucratic efficiency, few distractions and great coffee will take you a long way.

Don't compete, cooperate[13]

There is no more powerful belief in business than the one that vigorous competition leads to success. It is embedded in economic

---

[13] Parts of this section are taken from Delves Broughton, P., 'Joined-up thinking', *The Financial Times*, 8 June 2011. © The Financial Times Limited 2011. All rights reserved. For the full article, see the appendix at the back of the book.

and management theories, investment models and motivational speeches and, for some companies, is part of how they do business.

But a persuasive new set of theories is emerging, arguing that cooperation trumps competition. The fittest do not survive merely by outrunning their rivals. Rather, they win by finding ways to work together, by building the systems of trust and cooperation that allow groups to flourish.

> the fittest do not survive merely by outrunning their rivals

This may be hard for many business people to swallow, given how embedded their competitive instincts have become. In their book *SuperCooperators*, Martin Nowak, a Harvard professor of biology and mathematics, and Roger Highfield, a former editor of the *New Scientist* magazine, argue that the winners in life are those who resist the temptation to escalate conflicts. The losers punish others and perish as a result.

Their argument rests on Prof. Nowak's study of evolutionary principles which develops Charles Darwin's famous views. Humans are 'supercooperators', they say, because we manifest selfless behaviour that results from natural selection. We advance as a species not by beating each other, but rather by trusting each other and working together. This explains why ants build their colonies and humans build cities.

Applied to business, Prof. Nowak says 'the ultimate lesson is that it is co-operation, not competition, that underpins innovation. To spur creativity, and to encourage people to come up with original ideas, you need to use the lure of the carrot, not fear of the stick … Without co-operation, there can be neither construction nor complexity.'

Cooperation in business, however, can take many forms. Employees within a single organisation might cooperate to achieve shared goals. Or companies can cooperate with each other to dominate a market. And cooperation and competition are often not antithetical, but can be mutually supporting. By cooperating, for example, a company's employees might trounce their competitor. 'If at one bank, everyone is cut-throat, and at another everyone is collaborating, over time the collaborators will win', says Prof. Nowak.

The Harvard Business School academics Clay Christensen, Matt Marx and Howard Stevenson have written that there are various ways to persuade people within an organisation to set aside their competitive instincts and cooperate.[14] The key for a manager is to gauge how strongly his employees agree on where to go and the means of getting there. Then, he can use one of four sets of tools to get them to collaborate: power, management, leadership or culture.

The four tools range from highly aggressive to a gentle chivvying along and the management challenge is to know when to use which device. Power tools such as coercion and threats are used when employees agree on neither goals nor means. Management tools, such as training and measurement, work when employees agree on the goal but not on how to get there. Leadership tools, such as speeches and big vision statements, work to elicit cooperation in a well-functioning organisation towards a new goal. Culture tools, such as emphasising tradition and employee involvement, are the softest of all and work in companies capable of managing themselves.

An extreme example of power leadership is the bank executive Jamie Dimon. Professors Christensen, Marx and Stevenson write that when Mr Dimon became CEO of JPMorgan Chase and acquired his former bank, Bank One, in 2004, he cut executive salaries by as much as 50 per cent, threatened branch managers with the sack if they failed to meet quota, and warned the IT division that if they didn't choose a single platform for the merged businesses' IT within six weeks, he would pick one himself.

---

[14] 'The Tools of Cooperation and Change', Clayton M. Christensen, Matt Marx and Howard H. Stevenson, *Harvard Business Review*, 84, No. 10, October 2006

Starbucks' chief executive Howard Schultz used both power and leadership tools when he returned to the company he founded as chief executive in 2008. He employed the first when he closed stores and fired thousands of employees. Once he had got the company back into shape, he then wrote *Onward: How Starbucks Fought for its Life without Losing its Soul* to explain himself and act as a leadership tool to rally his battered troops.

The trick for managers is to get the balance right. It takes a particular blend of cooperation and competition to rise to the top of a large organisation. Even the most competitive individual requires the support of others to succeed. But cooperate too much, and you risk being taken advantage of by others.

Mark Weber of the University of Waterloo and J. Keith Murnighan of Northwestern University have written that the people who always volunteer and rally teams to overcome problems are invaluable to companies, but are treated as suckers for not pursuing their own interests.[15] In larger companies, says Prof. Murnighan, 'it's harder now for consistent co-operators to benefit from their actions. The consistent co-operator gets burnt once, and it takes a strong character to come back from that.'

As companies change more quickly and employees come and go with greater frequency, it is harder than ever to reap the long-term rewards of collaboration. Everyone is operating on a shorter time horizon, which leads to more self-interested behaviour.

Bruce Henderson, founder of the Boston Consulting Group, wrote an article in 1967 titled 'Brinkmanship in Business', which he said could equally be titled 'How to Succeed in Business by Being Unreasonable'.[16] He wrote that to compete effectively, it was

---

[15] 'Suckers or Saviors? Consistent Contributors in Social Dilemmas', J. Mark Weber and J. Keith Murnighan, *Journal of Personality and Social Psychology*, 95: 1340–53, 2008

[16] 'Brinkmanship in Business', B. Henderson, *Harvard Business Review*, March 1967

necessary to appear to be cooperating while in fact ensuring you get your own way. He compared business to international relations during peacetime, when countries compete ferociously but exercise restraint to avoid war. 'The goal of the hottest economic war', he wrote, 'is an agreement for coexistence, not annihilation.'

Some of the world's biggest industries exhibit just these alternating patterns of competition and cooperation. Coca-Cola and Pepsi may seem in constant battle, but their duopoly allows them to limit market access by smaller rivals and maintain pricing. Microsoft and Intel may have made billions from their near dominance in personal computing, but it has not stopped them fighting over how to divide up the profits. They cooperate to create value, but compete to appropriate it.

> some of the biggest industries exhibit alternating patterns of competition and cooperation

Among venture capitalists and technology companies, the ugly term 'coopetition' has been coined to describe the overlapping ties between boards, investors, executives and employees. The word triggers the interest of anti-trust regulators, and is just the kind of euphemism that leads to trouble and confusion. Firms which pretend to compete, but in fact cooperate to keep out rivals and fix prices, are at risk of breaking laws against the creation of monopolies.

While collaboration within organisations may make them more effective, competition between them tends to serve the consumer best. Even then, says Prof. Nowak, it doesn't solve all problems. Banks, for example, left to compete among each other did what was best for themselves but allowed the financial system to crater in 2008. 'We will always have oscillations between co-operation and collaboration, up and down', he says. 'There's never an equilibrium.'

Managers often receive conflicting messages about coopera-tion and competition. What matters is the context. Pay attention to your short- and long-term needs, and the interests of your customers. Ultimately, their needs are what matters, whether you fulfil them by playing hardball with your employees and rivals, or competing to deliver the very best solutions.

Dealing with complainers

There are two basic kinds of complainer, both of which need to be dealt with by managers.

The first kind is the constructive complainer. This might be someone with technical or consumer knowledge who has noticed a flaw in your operations and wishes to bring it to your attention. The best of them will do so in a helpful way, raising the issue and proposing a way to fix it. Others, though, may simply grumble to their co-workers. It is the manager's job to give these kinds of complainers the confidence to approach him without fear of sanction. Their complaints will often lead to improvements and should be welcomed. Their ideas, which tend to be specific suggestions for improved technical or management processes, should be solicited and encouraged.

The second kind of complainer is destructive. These are the whiners who rubbish everything. The parking sucks, the cafeteria is awful, the pay is too low and every new initiative is just more corporate garbage. With these kinds of complainers, a manager needs to be more subtle and patient. One's first tendency might be to purge them from the system because they are spreading poison. And there will certainly be destructive complainers who are best fired quickly before they do serious damage.

But a good manager will take the time to sift through the destructive complainer's complaints, and decide which are relevant and which not. Perhaps the parking does suck, and the pay is too low. If so, what could be done about it? Do these complainers actually have a point? And if so, how might their gripes be managed?

Of course, it is impossible to keep everyone happy. But it is the job of the manager to get the best work out of people, whether they are happy or not. Sometimes complainers uncover those areas where small improvements might make a big difference. Better food and easier parking might seem trivial on the surface, but they can have a dramatic effect on employee morale.

Another point to be considered with these destructive complainers is that they can serve as safety valves within an organisation. The truth is that employees will always complain. Having one person who lets off steam noisily on behalf of everyone may be better than having everyone simmering away quietly and resentfully.

> a destructive complainer can serve the same role as the fool in a medieval court

Provided they don't become toxic, a destructive complainer can serve the same role as the fool in a medieval court, mocking and speaking freely to the king, highlighting the truths which others with more to lose dare not speak.

Managing social networks

Lucky people don't rely on luck. They rely on opportunities, and those opportunities come to them through the people they know. They interact with large numbers of people and know how to make something of those interactions. 'Lucky people', wrote Dr Richard Wiseman, the author of *The Luck Factor* and an academic researcher of luck, 'are effective at building secure, and long-lasting, attachments with the people they meet. They are easy to know and most people like them. They tend to be trusting and form close relationships with others. As a result, they often keep in touch with a much larger number of friends and colleagues than unlucky people. And time and again this network of friends helps promote opportunity in their lives.'

For managers already trying to cope with employees whiling away their working hours on Facebook the idea of introducing a corporate social network may sound like insanity. What kind of gossip might appear on the internal message boards, which photographs on people's Walls? With companies already so paranoid about leaks or threats to their image, it seems an invitation to bad publicity.

But given how social networks have taken hold in our personal lives, it seems natural that their influence should spread into the corporate world. They are, after all, transforming how we communicate and share information online. Instant messaging within these networks is fast usurping email. Groups of people with common interests can now gather, share what they need, and disband with a few keystrokes. Finding a way to introduce the best of social networks into companies, while screening out the worst, has become a new and fast-growing niche for software vendors, and a challenge for managers.

With so many of us using social networks in our personal lives, it is inevitable that businesses take what is best about them and use them in their own operations. The benefits can also be huge. By mapping their company's social graph, its map of internal and external digital interactions, managers can gain a much deeper understanding of relationships, influence and the flows of significant information. Compared to this reward, the risk of a few ill-advised Wall posts about the office party pales into insignificance.

The first distinction managers must make is between personal and corporate networks. Personal networks may support photo sharing and games. Corporate networks, however, should be about relationship building and cooperation which lead to greater productivity. This may require a good deal of reminders to your employees. Once something is written and posted online, however secure the network, it could go anywhere. It may seem obvious, but employees need to be reminded of it time and again. Insurance companies nowadays have internal social networks where employees can discuss ongoing claims. This is not the place to recommend a good new place for lunch. It is the manager's job to make this point loudly and often. Once employees are clear on the guidelines for community networks, they tend to become self-policing.

> once something is written and posted online, it could go anywhere

A good example of how a social network might be used comes from Saatchi & Saatchi in the United States which has an 80-strong group handling advertising for the Toyota Dealers' Association in North America. Half of the group is based in New York, with the rest scattered across the country. They handle three major kinds of advertising – national, regional and dealer-specific – and are constantly juggling information ranging from creative work to production schedules and dealers' financial requirements. At first, people used their corporate social network as a substitute for instant messaging. But over time, they began to communicate more around certain projects and jobs, sharing local advertising plans and presentations. One of the surprisingly powerful aspects of the application was that each communication was accompanied by a smiling photograph of the sender. With a far-flung group, these photographs created a level of intimacy and understanding which had not existed before. But that is as far as the personal should go. Too much personal material can turn many people off. Keeping the network focused on business makes it clear what it is about and attracts more participants.

The companies most attracted to these new networks tend to be those undergoing rapid change, or which need to be in constant communication with their customers, such as those in retail, high-tech, consumer products and communications. Companies with younger workers, who already communicate via Facebook or on mobile devices, are also finding these networks useful, and quickly adopted. If successfully deployed and overseen by managers, they can create a tight weave of communication, which in turn leads to that coveted state of continuous learning.

But again, clear distinctions must be made between those networks which are for work and those for personal use. Whiling away the day reading friends' posts on Facebook is not a useful way for any employee to spend their day. But using social tools to collaborate on professional projects can vastly improve efficiency.

Managing performance

As we saw in the case of Google, managing performance is not a good thing in and of itself. The purpose of managing performance is to achieve specific organisational goals. The manager has no interest in a particular worker doing stellar work in an area of no significance for the business. This is not school, after all, where teachers are interested in helping you find your passion, or learning to learn. You are hired to do a particular job and if you don't do it, or if your contribution fails to help achieve a business goal, you become useless.

So rather than thinking about measuring performance, you should think instead of measuring usefulness. Two questions are essential to any usefulness measurement system. Both are focused on the future. The first is: what can I do about this situation? The second is: what can the person I manage do?

In any organisation, an individual's performance depends on their own wit and hard work and the tools they are given to succeed. The smartest, hardest-working salesman cannot succeed if his product is awful, his support lame and his manager idle and unresponsive. A performance review which accuses him of failing to achieve his targets is laying blame in the wrong place.

The first step for the manager, then, is to ask a few questions of yourself. Have you been doing all you can to help and monitor this employee along the way? Do you control the levers which could help this employee in the future? Are the metrics you have for this employee the right ones, and to what extent have external factors beyond the control of either of you affected his performance?

It is also worth asking what you might do to help an employee who is struggling. In some cases, their problems might be unfixable, or fixable only at an impossibly high cost. A salesperson who is scared of social situations may need extensive therapy to recover. But one who just needs a new car can easily be helped.

When meeting an employee, it is important to offer feedback which is specific, timely and action-oriented. There is nothing more maddening for an employee to be told that something they did weeks ago was wrong. Or indeed that they are doing something like 'sending out the wrong signals' without a very clear example of what you mean. Such lazy feedback also risks opening you to accusations of unreasonable prejudice.

Case Study

In 2001, the CEO of Cerner, an American medical software company based in Kansas, exploded in an email to his managers. He complained that many of his employees were working for less than 40 hours a week. He was appalled to see the car park nearly empty at 8 am and 5 pm. He told his managers: 'You have created expectations on the work effort which allowed this to happen inside Cerner, creating a very unhealthy environment. In either case, you have a problem and you will fix it or I will replace you. NEVER in my career have I allowed a team which worked for me to think they had a 40 hour job. I have allowed YOU to create a culture which is permitting this. NO LONGER.' He announced he was cutting jobs, demanding that employees punch in and punch out to work like factory workers, and suspending plans for any extra ▶

benefits. He said that from now on he would measure effort by the number of cars he saw in the parking lot early in the morning, late at night and at weekends. He wanted to see pizzas being delivered to evening meetings. 'I know the parking lot is not a great measurement for "effort". I know that "results" is what counts, not "effort". But I am through with the debate. We have a big vision. It will require a big effort. Folks this is a management problem, not an EMPLOYEE problem. Congratulations, you are management. You have the responsibility for our EMPLOYEES. I will hold you accountable. You have allowed this to get to this state. You have two weeks. Tick, tock.'

Cerner's stock price fell sharply when the email was leaked, before eventually recovering. What was great about the email, though, was that it was impassioned and unmistakably clear. Performance would now be measured according to one very tangible yardstick, cars in the car park, and managers would be held accountable.

You may not wish to go quite so far in your own communications, but the clarity of this message is worth consideration.

Appraisals must focus on specific goals and progress towards meeting them.

Start any performance appraisal by explaining its purpose in terms of goals and progress, then give the person being appraised a chance to talk without interruption. Let them explain what is going right, and give their reasons for anything going wrong. Once these are clear, you can then dig deeper to offer suggestions and help. What you are hoping to identify are the root causes for any gaps between expectation and performance, so that you can then lay out specific timelines and paths of action to reduce them. This needs to be recorded by both you, the manager, and the person being appraised, so that you can follow up on an agreed date. Appraisals need not be sources of fear or confrontation if they are conducted in this spirit of partnership and shared problem solving, rather than praise or blame.

Managers will always experience a tension between their roles as evaluators of their employees and as developers. A parent can focus on a child's development without ever having to worry about hiring or firing them. Managers don't have this luxury. They are expected to care about an employee's development, while also bearing in mind the employee's cost and usefulness.

If an employee is not performing, they must punish them in some way, by passing them over for promotion, demoting them or even firing them entirely. If this does come to pass, the manager will have done his job if the punishment comes as no surprise to the employee.

A fair measurement system gives the manager every chance to help the employee change and improve, and also keeps the employee posted on how his efforts are going. If for any reason, an employee does have to be fired, it will rarely be pleasant. They will inevitably accuse you of being unfair or not having given them fair warning. But a healthy and frequent appraisal system will mitigate these risks. Eventually.

So rather than waiting all year for that looming one-to-one formal, corporate appraisal with each of your employees, keep communicating with them all year. It will eliminate a lot of stress on both sides and allow you to intervene in order to help employees when they need it rather than waiting until the appraisal to discover a serious problem.

Dismissing staff

The first step in any dismissal process is to consult your company lawyer. Wrongful or badly handled dismissals will tarnish your own reputation and that of your company.

Once the legal requirements are clear, it is best to be direct with whomever you are dismissing. Tell them at the start of the conversation that you are dismissing them and give them the terms of their dismissal.

There are two broad categories of dismissal a manager must deal with. Those demanded at a corporate level for reasons beyond your control, such as a need to reduce head count. And those which employees bring on themselves, by dint of poor performance or misbehaviour. In either case, avoid siding with the employee against your company, or saying anything which could be used in any subsequent legal challenge. Be truthful about the reasons for dismissal.

> try if you can to dismiss people on a Monday

And try if you can to dismiss people on a Monday. That way they have the rest of the week to look for a new job. Handling dismissals is like opening bills. Avoid doing it on a Friday evening as it ruins everyone's weekend.

Earning trust

Trust is a vital lubricant in any management system. Without it everything takes much longer. Each action will require acts of self-preservation, emails being 'cc'd', forms and disclosures being signed. But when employees and managers trust each other both steady-state management and innovation can zip right along. An atmosphere of sharing and collaboration takes hold. People are not afraid to share ideas. Nor do they fear that a single misstep or ill-advised word will sink their careers. Companies often talk about the need for openness or transparency. What all this talk gets to is this need for trust, the engine oil of successful businesses.

Trust is an expression of confidence. If employees, suppliers and customers feel confident that you will do what you say, that you will keep your promises, pay your bills and deliver what it says on the box, then you have created trust. A lack of trust leads to a reluctance to cooperate, which can impose considerable costs on any organisation. Employees are constantly looking for other opportunities because they fear that management only cares about itself. Suppliers won't offer top-notch service because you cannot be trusted to pay when you say you will. And customers will leave at the first chance they have because they feel no loyalty.

Trust is the cheapest way to enable cooperative behaviour which in turn enables any organisation to get on with more interesting things, such as innovation and sales. The time and expense of monitoring and drafting minutely detailed contracts can be dramatically reduced if those you manage trust you and each other. It also makes the workplace more attractive.

Trust, however, is not easy to create and maintain. Many people regard trust as reckless. They feel exposed by trust and would rather shield themselves with distrustful procedures. They fear that it will lead inevitably to betrayal.

Social scientists have shown that in advanced, industrialised democracies since the 1960s, we have seen a dramatic erosion of trust, in all of our major social institutions, from businesses to the church and government. Perhaps we used to expect too much of them. But each time we see a politician disgraced, a business scandal exposed, or any of the once-trusted pillars of society collapse beneath us, we all trust a little less. In every case, it is the manager who is blamed, the person on top who should have known better, who betrayed all those beneath. The captain of a sinking ship must carry the can for the entire crew.

The manager is even blamed when problems are not their fault. There is little the manager of a Western manufacturing plant can do when his government decides to sign a trade agreement which allows a flood of cheap imports, and lets companies seek out cheaper suppliers elsewhere. The inexorable speed and rise of new technologies will make certain businesses obsolete before even the most agile manager can adapt. But whenever this happens, the manager will be seen to have failed. He was trusted and he failed.

Intense competition exacerbates suspicion rather than trust. In a brutally competitive marketplace, we often see acts of extreme cynicism being highly rewarded. How often do we hear of good guys finishing first? More often, it seems, it is the sharpest-elbowed, the most self-interested, the most suspicious-minded who wins. We see shareholders putting their interests over those of employees, or senior executives being handsomely rewarded for putting lifetime workers out to pasture.

Often this attitude is explained away by managers who say 'this is business, not personal'. Of course, for those on the rough end, it is always intensely personal. Scholars, such as Edward Freeman, call this separation of business from our everyday ethics and morality the 'separatist principle'. Its name hardly matters. What any manager must bear in mind is this constant battle between the need to succeed in the market, with the need to act in a decent manner.

One group of consultants might tell you that companies in which everyone trusts each other are those which do best. Another will say you need a spirit of ruthless competition in order to succeed. A third might say that you cannot always afford to keep your promises. At different times, in different situations, all might be right.

There are two kinds of factor which affect trust in an organisation. The first are personal, and relate to each individual's tolerance for risk, their level of self-confidence, and their position of power. Someone with high risk-tolerance, lots of self-confidence and in a powerful position is much more likely to trust people to get things done. Subordinates who fear for their jobs and hate change and risk tend to be less trusting.

The second set of factors relate to the situation in which you find yourself. In a company which is extremely profitable and has an entrenched and growing position in the market, people tend to be happier and more trusting. Where employees see each other as similar, or part of a tribe, they cut each other more slack. The same when people feel they are all in it together. If they feel that their actions will lead to justly shared rewards or punishments, they tend to act in harmony. We trust people we believe are highly capable,

> we trust those we believe are highly capable of doing what they promise

because they have a good track record of doing what they promise or overcoming challenges, as well as those we think have our interests at heart. And finally, we believe in those who are straight with us, who tell us what we deserve to know, good or bad. Lies, distortions and poor communication can easily destroy trust.

Break this down even further, and we can see that when we trust a manager, we don't simply trust those we think are good people. We trust those we believe are capable of doing what they promise. Those we think share and will serve our interests. We trust an airline pilot not because of how he behaved towards his colleagues yesterday, but because he has been trained to fly the plane, and if he does it poorly, his life is as much at risk as ours.

For a manager to be worthy of trust, then, he must not just possess good values and good intentions, but also the executional ability to turn those values and intentions into actions which enhance the lives of all those he deals with each day. If he can inspire that trust, it will seep into every area of the organisation he touches.

The first step to inspiring trust is to let your reports know who you are. This does not require an embarrassing act of improper self-revelation. Rather, you must give them any information they might need to trust you. If you wish to manage them towards taking more risks, you must demonstrate your own capacity to tolerate and manage risk. Provide evidence of your competence and experience. Explain your own career path, perhaps, or your personal situation if necessary. Anything you feel is relevant to increasing the confidence of those you manage. Any information you choose to disclose should help them reach a point where they can trust you to do what is right for them.

If you are managing a thousand shop-floor mechanics, they have no need to know that you have three children and a mortgage.

What they need to know is that you are doing all you can to ensure their jobs are secure, their workplace is safe and that you are a competent defender of their interests. If your team consists of four creatives at an advertising agency, they might need to know that you can argue for their ideas, that you will stand up for them against the 'suits', and that you grasp that the creative process is not always linear. You win their trust by enabling them to do their best work and ensuring that it is amply rewarded.

Managers who set up secretive compensation schemes which reward them for punishing their employees will, if discovered, lose any trust. But a manager who is rewarded when his reports perform well will earn their trust.

It is also worth considering the gruesome consequences when trust breaks down. Once trust collapsed at Enron, it destroyed its trading business. The facts which kept emerging were worse than anyone in management had admitted. Right up until its collapse, Enron's senior executives were asserting that they had created 'the right company with the right model at the right time'. They boasted about their 'well-established business approach and innovative people'. Neither could save the company from its own criminality.

A good reason to stop trusting a manager and an organisation is when what they say starts to sound unnecessarily complex. Complexity is often a cover for weakness or worse. Conflicts of interest and poor incentives also provide fuel for untrustworthy behaviour. Arthur Andersen was earning more from selling its consulting services to Enron than it was selling its audit services. Unsurprisingly, the audits were not conducted with proper rigour, for fear of losing the consulting business. As Sherron Watkins, the woman who ultimately blew the whistle on Enron, said, 'I've come to the sad conclusion that when a lot of money is pouring on top of your head, it really clouds your judgment.'

Renaissance sages kept a skull on their desks to remind them of their own mortality. Managers, especially those experiencing a period of success, would do well to do the same, and recall that the basis of success is trust in their competence and it doesn't take much to destroy that.

Nurturing creativity

When set against the infinite variety of human motivations, management incentives can seem woefully crude. Businesses want to elicit certain outcomes, which lead to sustained profitability, but to do so they must battle their way through the full range of human mental states and behaviours, from excitement to boredom, extreme creativity to stultifying rule-following. We do, however, know a few things. For example, that when you want people to do their most creative work, they need to find powerful internal reasons, or 'intrinsic motivations', for doing so. Offering more money, perks or promotions, 'extrinsic motivations', may help get a task completed on time, but in order to get the creative juices flowing, people have to be inclined to do the work for reasons they find personally inspiring and meaningful. On the other hand, ignoring the 'extrinsic motivations' is no use either, as no one wants to feel taken advantage of.[17]

Finding the correct balance for each of your employees is an on-going challenge for managers. Some will go to any lengths for a pay rise. Others will do their best work only when they feel it is highly valued for its creativity or contribution to a difficult solution. Some will be happy with a new job title, others will care nothing for titles and only want the respect and approval of their peers. Some value their social position, others covet a profound feeling of competence. The ideal timing for each kind of motivation may also vary. Keeping a loose schedule early in the process may help people relax and find creative solutions, but imposing a deadline later on may force them to be rigorous and deliver their best work.

---

[17] 'How to Kill Creativity', Teresa M. Amabile, *Harvard Business Review*, September–October 1998

The greatest stimulant to creativity is interesting, challenging work. In sports, most people want to play opponents a little better than themselves, as it improves their own game. So it is with ambitious workers. They want to get better at whatever it is they do. Matching the right work to the right person is a manager's job. You can either make the match yourself, based on your own observations, or invite volunteers to take on new projects.

You then want to think hard about the time and money you plan to assign to the project, and the extent you wish to manage it. You want to give workers enough time and money so they can accomplish the work to their best ability, but not so much they dawdle or become wasteful. Similarly, you want to give them sufficient autonomy so they feel ownership of the process and can decide how best to apply their talents to the problem, but also enough guidelines so they have a clear goal in mind and don't feel lost amidst all the options too much autonomy can provide.

Managers must recognise that when they ask employees to be creative, they are asking them to take a risk and expose themselves. The worst thing they can possibly do is fail to respect that risk, by criticising work too early or not even responding to it at all. Managers and organisations rarely get a second or third try at inspiring creativity. Once employees feel that it is too risky for them to embark on a 'creative' process, because it will be ignored or laughed down before it is completed, they won't ever take the risk of exposing themselves in this way. Ambitious employees tend to criticise rather than praise the work of others in order to seem cleverer than their bosses. But this is utterly toxic for creativity and managers must be aggressive in stopping this pattern emerging. They must be clear about their own understanding of the creative process: that it will involve more failures than successes, that it is a process which demands and accepts constant adjustment and iteration along the way, but that ultimately, when harnessed to discipline and hard work, it is the surest way to long-term success.

Top 10 tips for managing others

1 People are drawn to cultures as much as companies.

2 Monitor and measure all you can, but keep an open door to bring humanity to the numbers.

3 Hire for potential not for achievements past.

4 Hire to get specific tasks done and goals met, not for a personality type.

5 There are people who know what to do, people who know how to do it, and people who can persuade others to come along with them. Hiring is not the same for each group.

6 Identify how you and your organisation rely on stereotypes when hiring and try actively to find candidates who challenge your notion of the 'right' hire.

7 Even when managing a team, you are still managing individuals with very different motivations and needs.

8 Teams need both collaboration and conflict to succeed. Collaboration to enable work to happen, conflict to ensure poor ideas or effort are not left unchallenged.

9 Smart people will always see through meaningless corporate jargon. Don't even try it.

10 Recognise what else it is people work for, besides their pay cheque.

Chapter 3
Managing processes

What topics are covered in this chapter?

- Learning to be lean
- Communicating your ideas effectively
- Getting the most out of meetings
- Influencing and negotiating
- Enabling innovation

I n 1952, the British Alpine Club and the Royal Geographical Society received shocking news. A Swiss expedition had come within a few hundred feet of the summit of Mount Everest. For years the British had regarded the conquest of the world's highest peak as theirs to achieve. The prospect of a team from another country conquering 'their' mountain was sobering. The Nepalese government had taken to limiting attempts on Everest to one per year. The British had their turn in 1953. In 1954, it would be the French and in 1955, the Swiss again. For the British, it was 1953 or never.

The greatest British climber at the time was Eric Shipton, a climber's climber who knew the Himalayas better than anyone. But when the Alpine Club met in London to consider the challenge in 1953, they decided that what the expedition needed was not just a great climber. It needed a great manager.

They turned to John Hunt. Hunt was an accomplished climber in his own right, but nothing like Shipton. More importantly, he had distinguished himself during the Second World War as a formidable organiser. He served as chief instructor at the Commando Mountain and Snow Warfare School and led troops in bitter fighting in Italy and Greece. After the war, he had served in senior staff appointments in the Middle East and the Supreme Headquarters Allied Expeditionary Force. He was a man who could get things done.

At 42, he was considered old for such a gruelling expedition and his appointment infuriated many of the more seasoned climbers, who favoured Shipton. But he dug in and quickly won round his men. He viewed the ascent as more than a physical or technical challenge. It was also an organisational challenge, which would require diligent planning and execution. It was a process which would demand all of his managerial talent. 'The ascent of Everest was not the work of one day, nor even of those few anxious, unforgettable weeks last spring in which we prepared and climbed the mountain', he wrote. 'It is, in fact, a tale of sustained and tenacious endeavour by many, over a long period of time.'[1]

He began by studying the nature of the challenge. The climbing, he concluded, was only part of it. Previous expeditions had failed because of a lack of oxygen or supplies at crucial moments up the mountain. It was not only important to pick the right men, a gifted, tenacious and compatible group, but also to equip and supply them properly. He faced the additional challenges of financing the expedition and pulling it off within a short time.

In recruiting climbers, he sought two qualities above all else: a strong individual desire to reach the summit, the 'Excelsior' spirit, the desire to go ever higher; and extraordinary selflessness and patience. Such qualities were rarely found in the same individual, but Hunt felt they were vital to creating a unified, spirited party.

He broke the effort down into separate challenges: training; timing, giving the expedition the most time possible to climb before the monsoon; minimising the time spent high up the mountain; making the most of the time available; ensuring a proper supply of oxygen; and the limits placed by the terrain on moving supplies up the mountain. Hunt left no detail to chance, from the weight of the climbers' boots, tents and cooking stoves to diet and liquid intake.

---

[1] *The Conquest of Everest*, Sir John Hunt, E.P. Dutton and Company, 1953

He challenged even the most basic assumptions. Previous expeditions had carried food in bulk stores. Hunt's team broke their food down into ration packs, conforming closely to the European diet. By packing food in 'man-day units' he hoped to reduce the likelihood of pilfering, which happened frequently with bulk stores, reduce contamination through excessive handling and increase efficiency by transporting only what was necessary. His medical team even foresaw the likelihood of boredom with these rations, and included 'luxury boxes' containing items chosen by the climbers themselves while they were in England, ranging from pineapple chunks and Marmite to rum and Cheddar cheese.

As the party moved up the mountain, Hunt used a system of relays, moving supplies up and establishing camps before following up with the rest of the team. It all culminated with Edmund Hillary and Tenzing Norgay reaching the summit on 29 May 1953.

As Hunt reflected on the expedition, he attributed its success to learning from other expeditions and to 'sound, thorough, meticulously detailed planning'. On Everest, he wrote, 'the problems of organisation assume the proportions of a military campaign; I make no apology for this comparison, or for the fact that we planned the ascent of Everest on these lines. It was thanks to this that we were able not only to foresee our needs in every detail – guided by previous experience provided by others, we judged aright – but to have constantly before us a clear programme to carry out at every stage: the march-out; acclimatisation; preparation of the Icefall; the first and second stages of the build-up; reconnaissance and preparation of the Lhotse Face; even, in outline, the assault plan itself. These were the aims to be achieved by given dates, and achieve each and all of them we would, and did.'

That final sentence should be pinned to the wall of every manager in business and elsewhere.

Learning from Toyota's production system

The most famous industrial production system in the world is Toyota's. It is a masterpiece of efficiency which helped Toyota become the world's largest producer of motor vehicles. Such has been Toyota's success that almost all of its competitors, and many other industrial companies, have sought to replicate its system. The problem for these copycats has been grasping that in the Toyota system, rigidity, specification and repetition work hand in hand with creativity and adaptability. There are strictly enforced routines at Toyota, but these are designed to do two seemingly contradictory things: create uniformly excellent products; and allow constant tinkering by employees, managers and suppliers.[2]

The most dramatic difference between Toyota's production methods and those of other companies is their minute focus on detail. Other companies may think they are focused, but nothing like Toyota. For example, to install a right front seat in a Toyota Camry, for example, the work is broken down into a seven-step sequence which must be performed in 55 seconds as the car moves at an unchanging speed past a worker's station. The steps must be performed in the same order, in the same way in the same length of time. If even the slightest thing is out of sequence, then the worker and his manager know something is going wrong. As he moves along, the worker passes markers on the floor which provide visual aids to help him know if he is on or off schedule.

In order to ensure workers understand both how and why they work in this fashion, managers are told not to prescribe work, but to ask questions and elicit answers from their employees. How do you do your work? How do you know you are doing it correctly? What do you do if something goes wrong? Once workers can answer these

---

[2] For a complete analysis of the Toyota system, see 'Decoding the DNA of the Toyota Production System', Steven Spear and H. Kent Bowen, *Harvard Business Review*, October 1999

questions, they are felt to have a real grasp of what they do. As they perform the routines of their work each day, they are encouraged to keep asking themselves if this is the right way to do each job, to test each method as a scientist would test a hypothesis.

This emphasis on total clarity extends to how people communicate with each other and how they report problems. Every human interaction is carefully defined at Toyota so that employees know who is responsible for what, whether it is delivering spare parts or helping solve a technical problem. The responsiveness of these interactions is then tested as compulsively as the assembly process. If a problem cannot be resolved or a part delivered in a specific number of seconds, then it suggests the interaction is poorly designed. Toyota has such confidence in this system that it encourages workers to ask for help the moment a problem arises. They don't fear that constant stopping and starting will gum up their production system, because the problem solving system is built in and is as efficient as the machine which bolts doors together.

At the heart of Toyota's production system is a profound faith in human intelligence. All of the teaching which goes on at the company, and it is omnipresent, is about turning each employee into their own centre of knowledge. Managers are expected to understand fully the work of each of their employees. And employees are expected to regard each day's work as a sophisticated laboratory experiment designed to search for flaws and potential improvements to the system. Every assumption at Toyota is there to be tested, and the best testers are the people who work there. This culture of continuous testing and searching for improvement means that workers must accept that the existing system is imperfect. What matters in such a system is not being able to point to a change and boast about it, but rather to regard the triumph as the practice of relentless change.

Visitors to Toyota's plants are often startled to see cords hanging along the production lines, which any employee can pull in order to stop the line. In other factories, stopping production is a privilege reserved for a senior manager. For Toyota, however, the cord is not what matters. More important is what the cord represents, an effort by the company to give employees their voice in improving the production system. There is no such thing as a permanent solution at Toyota, only what they call 'countermeasures'.

These countermeasures are all designed to help the production system work towards an ideal state, where there are no defects, where products can be customised to each customer, supplied on demand, produced without waste and in a plant which is safe and enjoyable for workers.

The myriad rules at Toyota are not designed to stifle employees, but rather to liberate them from chaos. By making clear rules about expectations and lines of command, Toyota aims to free its employees from bureaucratic confusion, and allow them to tinker with modular parts of the production system without upending the whole.

Managing an entire process can seem overwhelming. But any manager can follow Toyota's model by adopting a mindset of constant improvement over even the minutest detail, and welcoming the suggestions of employees which lead to incremental change.

Starting lean and staying lean

The influence of Toyota's famed production system has spread far beyond manufacturing. It has influenced software, where the concept of 'agile' software development, drawing on tightly coordinated networks to test, iterate and improve software as it is developed, is now commonly applied in large-scale projects. And since 2008, it has been taken up by Silicon Valley entrepreneurs and applied to start-ups. Even though Toyota suffered through a spate of recalls in 2010, and saw its reputation badly dented, its management principles are still revered.

At the core of Toyota's philosophy is the idea of 'lean' processes. The term is often misunderstood to mean cheap. In fact, a lean production system is one in which every step of every process is transparent and considered ripe for improvement. 'Thinking lean' is about constantly measuring all you do, and being able to change quickly as fresh evidence

> at the core of Toyota's philosophy is the idea of 'lean' processes

emerges. It is about streamlining processes in order to allow rapid adaptation in the discovery or start-up phase of a company, product or process.

Apply this to launching a new product within an existing company. The classic method is for managers to look at the market for an opportunity, establish a business case, develop a product, test, validate and finally launch. At each stage, the manager gathers resources, establishes criteria for the next step and tries to adjust as he goes. The challenge these days, though, is that technology and customer tastes are moving so fast that the classic method is no longer adequate.

Start-ups tend to be much higher-risk endeavours than they need to be. Entrepreneurs in every setting make the same mistakes. They build elaborate products before daring to test them with consumers. They make decisions based on the wrong information, and they stick with bad ideas long after they should. Their behaviour is supported by the entrepreneurial myths of innovators who persisted through endless rejection eventually to be validated by success. But it isn't necessary any more. This is a great example of an advance in management science and practice.

Eric Ries, a Silicon Valley entrepreneur who has coined the phrase 'lean start-ups', happens to drive a new Toyota. While he's delighted with the car, he says its GPS system encapsulates the problem. Here you have a car packed with technology, but the GPS system is primitive compared with what he could download to his phone. The reason is that the innovation cycle time for car manufacturing is much slower than that for GPS software. So one part of the car will seem dated long before the rest of it.

Ries hit on the idea of lean start-ups after suffering one failed technology start-up and enjoying one success, the instant messaging company IMVU, as well as observing the peculiar fortunes of many others as an investor and adviser. The classic start-up methods, built on linear management and innovation processes, he found, were not working for him or his peers. 'They kept blowing up in my face', he says.

Such methods offered too little flexibility to deal with changes in available technology and in customer needs. Imagine that today you decide to launch a new product. You seize the opportunity, talk to potential customers, gather the resources and set to work. By the time you're ready to launch, what are the chances your product is still relevant?

Ries defines a start-up as a 'human institution designed to create a new product or service under conditions of extreme uncertainty'. The words 'human' and 'uncertainty' are essential to what follows. A successful start-up does not just rely on a brilliant idea, but also requires managing people through all the challenges of innovation and growth, and through times when the idea will fail and when people will fight over what to do next.

Ries and other new management thinkers – notably Steve Blank, a former entrepreneur who now teaches classes at Stanford and the Haas School of Business at Berkeley – say the risks in any start-up can be reduced by constant interaction with potential customers during product development. As noted in the last section, by keeping each step of any process small and opening it up to feedback, you can quickly correct mistakes and make improvements.

When it comes to the critical issue of when and how to change strategic direction, some in the organisation will want to persevere on a prescribed route, while others will want to change direction entirely. Useful data will be vital to making the decision based on reason rather than emotion. Lean practices, like all the best management practices, seek out relevant numbers to help with decision making. Go beyond pure revenue to look at customer adoption, retention and usage patterns to help decide which way to go. It will help make any strategic 'pivots' much easier to make, as they will require less blind courage and more reason.

Technology companies are the most obvious seeding ground for these ideas. Facebook began with profile pages and a basic messaging service and has been adding features over time based on feedback from users. But the ideas are equally applicable to larger companies. Ries has advised multinationals around the world on their innovation processes. 'My own definition of a start-up is an institution asked to create something new under conditions of high uncertainty', he says. 'This has nothing to do with company size.'

One counter-argument to this is that some risks are better taken than minimised. Customer development may increase your chances of certain revenue, but not your chances of maximum revenue. Great product innovators, like great film-makers or novelists, can develop in isolation, deposit their products on an unsuspecting market and still triumph. But that is a high-risk route. For the more ordinary among us lean is a far better way to go.

Jeff Bezos, the founder and chief executive of Amazon, believes firmly in trying new things and encourages his employees to do the same thing, to 'go down blind alleys', in the knowledge that 'every once in a while, you go down an alley and it opens up into this huge, broad avenue'.[3] This approach has produced dramatic misfires, such as a program to show each shopper customers with matching buying profiles, and hits, such as the Affiliates program, which pays other websites a royalty on purchases they've directly driven to Amazon.

---

[3] 'Jeff Bezos: Blind Alley Explorer', Robert Hof, *Business Week*, 19 August 2004

To take this approach to innovation requires managerial confidence and a comfort with improvisation and uncertainty which sits at odds with standard managerial procedures. Imagine two cooks going into a kitchen. One goes to their own, familiar kitchen, reaches immediately for the recipe book, decides on a meal and then sets about assembling the ingredients and scribbling down measurements and timings before starting work. This is the classic, linear, managerial approach in which the goal is set and steps taken to achieve it. Another cook asked to make a meal is quite happy entering an unfamiliar kitchen, seeing what is in the cupboards and then doing his best with what is there. The result could be disgusting or delicious, and will certainly be less predictable. But the chef in this second scenario will undoubtedly learn more than the first. The first approach works well when everything is known. The second works better when you are dealing with the unknown.[4]

Military strategists call this incremental, learning by doing approach 'developing the situation through action'. It does not imply unpreparedness. Quite the opposite. It requires you do all the preparation you can, but then remain ready to adapt in the face of reality. This approach was central to the counter-insurgency strategy of the US military in Iraq, adopted after several years of rigorous top-down planning had failed. Soldiers were no longer told that the tried and true methods were gospel, but rather to reconnoitre and discover what would work, to improvise and adapt in the face of a mobile, amorphous enemy. They were encouraged to make mistakes and learn from them.[5]

> do all the preparation you can, but then remain ready to adapt

[4] 'What Makes Entrepreneurs Entrepreneurial', Saras Sarasvathy, University of Washington, 2001

[5] 'Systematic Operational Design: Learning and Adapting in Complex Missions', Brigadier General Huba Wass de Czege, US Army Retired, *Military Review*, January–February 2009

Vinod Khosla, the co-founder of Sun Microsystems, and a successful Silicon Valley investor, said of the entrepreneurial approach: 'I believe in bumbling around long enough to not give up at anything. And eventually success comes your way, because you tried to fail in every possible way, the only way that's left is the one successful way, which always, for entrepreneurs, seems to come last. It's so obvious when it comes.'[6]

Big companies have seized on this 'fail quickly – learn quickly' approach. In 2001, Procter & Gamble, which owns two dozen billion-dollar consumer products brands, introduced a prototyping approach to its products, encouraging its team to create basic versions of what they had in mind and testing them early with customers.

These versions might be held together with tape and glue, but they had the invaluable impact of eliciting much more honest feedback than products which were more fully developed. People were more willing to tell the truth than they were when they felt huge amounts of resources had already been invested. It allowed the company to adapt much earlier in the product development process.

At Pixar, the animation studio which created hits such as *Finding Nemo* and *Cars*, the teams of animators have a process called 'plussing'. When an animator has done a set of drawings, they bring them in to a meeting with the director. The director does not say 'yes' or 'no' at this point, but rather seizes on something he does like and says, 'and how about we also do this . . .'.

Any manager can do the same, seeking to influence without seeming to judge. By getting into processes early and staying involved, he and his team can keep adding positives all along the way rather than waiting to deliver either praise or a deflating

---

[6] 'Vinod Khosla: How to Succeed in Silicon Valley by Bumbling and Failing ...', *Silicon Valley Watcher*, 28 June 2009

raspberry once all the work has been done. It helps avoid the dreaded 'HiPPO' phenomenon, in which the 'highest-paid person's opinion' dominates every discussion.

Another technique, with the same purposes of encouragement, efficiency and minimising risk while maximising innovation, is called 'smallifying'. This is especially popular with software developers but can be used in many other settings. It involves breaking down large tasks into unique problems which can be solved in one or two weeks. By making work less daunting and overwhelming, managers can unleash their employees' creativity. This idea came from Japanese manufacturing, where companies like Honda deployed small cross-functional teams, made of designers, engineers, production experts and sales teams, to drive a process forward, project by project. This was the antithesis of the General Motors approach, which specified tasks to be performed by functional experts, before integrating them all at the end.

Case Study

At Alcoholics Anonymous, recovering drinkers are not advised to give up drinking for ever. They are told to focus on not drinking today. Conquer temptation for the next hour and then the next 24 hours. If you do that, then eventually you will put together consecutive days of not drinking, and with the accumulation of small victories you will have the base for more and larger wins.

For managers, winning small can establish a habit of doing things properly and emerging victorious.

Death by PowerPoint: Sharing information

When Steve Jobs returned to run Apple in 1997, he despaired of the number of people who came into meetings determined to show him PowerPoint presentations. 'I hate the way people use slide presentations instead of thinking', he said. 'People would confront a problem by creating a presentation. I wanted them to engage, to hash things out at the table, rather than show a bunch of slides. People who know what they're talking about don't need PowerPoint.'

Anyone who has suffered the intellectual indignity of PowerPoint knows what he means. Slide upon slide of empty bullet points and massaged numbers, accompanied by garish images, twirling icons fading in and out of view. The 'death by PowerPoint' involves hours spent in conference rooms witnessing a presentation padded out to the allotted time as supposed evidence of work.

Young management consultants do almost nothing but prepare decks of PowerPoint slides for their bosses to use to bludgeon clients into corporate re-engineering. But what's simply a waste of time and money in the corporate world becomes even more dangerous when applied to, say, fighting the 'war on terror'.

The US military finally revolted against the choking effect of PowerPoint after a slide designed to show generals the complexity of America's military strategy in Afghanistan went viral. On first seeing it, General Stanley McChrystal, then leader of US forces in Afghanistan, remarked: 'When we understand that slide, we'll have won the war.'

Another general told *The New York Times* that 'PowerPoint makes us stupid', while another said the software is 'dangerous because it can create the illusion of understanding and the illusion of control. Some problems in the world are not bullet-izable.' There is even an Anti-PowerPoint political party in Switzerland which claims that PowerPoint presentations waste 350 billion euros' worth of time around the world each year.

The main arguments against PowerPoint are that it relieves the presenter of the need to deliver analytic argument. Charts are often built with aesthetic rather than factual considerations in mind. The military even joke that the best use of it is in numbing reporters into submission. They call the style of these presentations 'hypnotising chickens'. Edward Tufte, a Yale professor hired by President Obama to improve how the White House presents information graphically, is one of PowerPoint's greatest foes. He has modified Lord Acton's remark about the corrosive effect of power, to say 'Power Corrupts. PowerPoint Corrupts Absolutely'.

In an essay on the subject, Tufte wrote: 'Imagine a widely used and expensive prescription drug that promised to make us beautiful but didn't. Instead the drug had frequent, serious side-effects: it induced stupidity, turned everyone into bores, wasted time, and degraded the quality and credibility of communication. These side-effects would rightly lead to a worldwide product recall.'

PowerPoint presents information in short, sequential bites, which inhibits cross-referencing. Compare that with a few rich tables of numerical data supplemented by a well-written analysis, which can then provide the basis for a discussion. The latter takes less time to absorb but requires the full involvement of the reader and is less likely to lead to facts being moulded to the format.

As Tufte puts it: 'The PowerPoint style routinely disrupts and dominates, and trivializes content. Thus PowerPoint presentations too often resemble a school play – very loud, very simple.'

Case Study

The US military found huge gaps between what people thought they had agreed to and what they actually decided on. An essay titled 'Dumb-dumb Bullets', published in 2009 by an ex-US Marine colonel, said PowerPoint allowed for vague statements such as 'accelerate the introduction of new weapons', which lead to nods around the room without specifying when, by whom and of what nature.[7] Much of the planning for the invasion of Iraq in

▶

---

[7] 'Dumb-dumb Bullets', T.X. Hammes, *Armed Forces Journal*, July 2009

2002 was done in PowerPoint. 'One excuse given for using PowerPoint is that senior leaders don't have time to be pre-briefed on all the decisions they make', wrote the colonel. 'If that is the case, they are involved in too many decisions. When the default position is that you are too busy to prepare properly to make a decision, it means you are making bad decisions.' It applies as well to the business world as it does to the military.

Not that it doesn't have its uses. PowerPoint is best used in delivering simple information but should be avoided as a means of presenting the argument for a decision. Use PowerPoint to provide an outline of your argument, then fill in the rest orally.

Old-fashioned flip charts are also often just as effective and more interactive. Audience members can come up and add their own comments much more easily with a marker pen on paper, than if they have to immerse themselves in the presenter's technology.

If you are going to present at a meeting, the best way is to give each person in the meeting a couple of sheets of paper detailing your main points. Then flesh them out when you speak, using either a flip chart, or slides which are very simple to read. Your audience can always ask questions if they need clarification. Your slides do not need to be comprehensive. You do.

Offering too much information will not only confuse and bore your audience, but will also lead some to think you either don't have a clear grasp of your work, or that you are trying to hide something.

It is quite common for people to send huge chunks of information attached to emails hoping people will read it. Chances are they won't. Think about digesting large amounts of information into a few short paragraphs or points, which can be easily printed out, then send it at times people are likely to read it, first thing in the morning perhaps, or at the end of the day, when their in-boxes are ticking over more slowly.

By making your messages clear and concise, you will not only get a better hearing, but you will be showing respect for people's time and energy.

Getting the most out of meetings

A curious application arrived in 2011 at the United States Patent Office from a group of software developers at IBM. They had asked themselves this question: why is it that so many meetings go on for an hour, when they could be shorter? The answer, they decided, was that this is the way most people break up their day. They arrange appointments to begin and end on the hour and coordinate their calendars and book conference rooms accordingly. It has nothing to do with the specific requirements of a meeting.

> why is it that many meetings go on for an hour, when they could be shorter?

IBM's solution is software which offers people a range of meeting times. If all you need is five minutes, or thirty-five, so be it. No need to invite people for the full hour. Everyone complains about meetings but here was a real attempt to reorganise the fundamental process by which they occur. When so much communication is electronic, face-to-face meetings remain vital. It's no use saying all meetings are awful. Some things will just never happen unless you look someone in the eye.

How you organise those meetings depends on the kind of operation you run. The classic bad meeting involves six or more people sitting around a conference table with no real agenda. Millions of hours of corporate time billow away in such pointless activity.

Everyone in business loves to complain about meetings, but they are a fact of life. One way to think of them is as the means by which managerial work gets done. No manager cannot meet with the people he is managing. So the best you can do is make your meetings as efficient and effective as possible.

One useful distinction is between meetings which deal with process, and meetings which deal with mission.[8] Process meetings include regularly scheduled one-on-ones with peers and subordinates, operations reviews and annual reports. Mission meetings are those held on an ad hoc basis which must lead to a decision. They answer questions like, how do we deal with this particular problem? What steps do we need to take now to fight this fire? What strategy shall we pursue this year?

The best you can do with any meeting is not waste people's time. You can help this by starting and finishing on time and by having a meeting summary template, consisting of the date, the invitees, a list of who came and who didn't, what was discussed, what was agreed on, and who was given the task of doing what by when.

In this way, meetings can become operational tools, a means of sharing information and assigning tasks and responsibilities rather than a waste of time. It also creates a system of process improvement. By keeping detailed records of who was invited and who came, for example, you can refine your list of invitees to ensure that you only invite and inform the relevant people about each meeting.

Simple but obvious measures can also squeeze the waste out of meetings. State the purpose of the meeting at the beginning and ask if everyone in the room needs to be there. If they stay, it is then their decision. If people are consistently late, find a way for people to acknowledge their rudeness without humiliating them by making them put money in a jar which is then given to charity.

Mix up the list of meeting invitees to get the right people in the room. All too often, managers try to protect their authority by not bringing in people lower down in their organisation who may know much more about a particular problem than they do.

---

[8] *High Output Management*, Andy Grove, Vintage, 1986

Factory workers will likely know more about the working of their machines than their managers. Software developers will know more about the technical feasibility of their work than those trying to market it. Bringing in experts helps eradicate the Chinese whispers effect on organisational knowledge, in which information gets more distorted the further it has to travel up or down a hierarchy.

Also include junior people who may have little to contribute now but will learn from watching how decisions are made and progress checked. Meetings can be an important classroom for younger employees, as they demystify why a company does what it does.

During meetings, ask the people who do the work what their solution would be. Don't expect them to speak without being asked.

Too much managerial time is spent looking for complex solutions, when a simple one might be staring you in the face. Any meeting can be made dramatically more effective by getting the right people there and asking their opinion.

A few other basic modifications can vastly improve the usefulness of meetings. The first is to recognise how different people need to structure their time. One distinction is between 'managers' and 'makers'. Managers tend to have many decisions to make during each day, lots of data to collect and a long checklist to work through. They need to move from one thing to another to get everything done.

Makers, however, work on longer projects and need larger chunks of time. A software developer, for example, may need entire days free of appointments and distractions to complete a project. Schedule a mid-morning meeting and their attention is shot. You wouldn't ask Damien Hirst to drop his brush and pop in for an hour's chat about his gallery's fee structure.

> there is no point in berating your staff in meetings ... when what they need is fewer meetings

There is no point berating your staff in meetings for not doing enough when what they need most is fewer meetings. With 'makers', it might be best only scheduling meetings in one half of the day, so that they have the other half clear to gain momentum in their work.

An American website called meetordie.com invites you to enter your industry, the length of your meeting and the number and roles of the participants. It then spits out an estimate of the amount of money being wasted by the meeting, and a suggestion for how it might be better spent. On drinking water for Africans, for example. Ricardo Semler, a Brazilian industrialist and author of *The Seven Day Weekend*, proposes not requiring anyone to show up to meetings. If you call one, and people come, the meeting is worthwhile. If no one comes, it tells you it was a waste of time in the first place.

Morning stand-up meetings are an efficient way of clearing a lot of business when everyone is still buzzing with caffeine and there aren't so many interruptions. A 10-minute get-together first thing, when marching orders are given and priorities set, can free people to gather in smaller groups later in the day if necessary. You can do this in a hallway, or in a room without chairs, so no one feels inclined to linger.

The only people who need to be at longer meetings are those who can affect its outcome. Those who can only act on a decision have no need to attend. Another idea, akin to IBM's, is the Swiss Federal Railways approach. Set very specific times and durations for meetings. Say they will begin at 10.12 am and finish at 10.26 am. Such specificity might bring people in on time and keep things moving on a tight schedule, leaving no time for the dreaded 'any other business'. Then break the meeting down into even smaller blocks, 90 seconds on this, 5 minutes on that, so nothing gets missed and people understand they cannot gas on. Don't allow diversions from the agenda. An even more radical idea is to adopt the Quaker approach of starting each meeting in silence and inviting anyone who has something to say to dare break it. Lots of thought. And few words. It helped the Quakers build companies from Cadbury to Barclays, and may be due a revival.

Mastering the art of negotiation

This is a subject worthy of volumes on its own. The book *Getting to Yes: Negotiating Agreement Without Giving In* by Roger Fisher and William Ury is a great place to start.

But there are a few basic things a manager needs to know in order to be a successful negotiator. The first, and most important, is to decide what kind of negotiator you are.

There are three basic types:

1 The poker player, who regards the negotiation purely as a game in which bluffing and other forms of deceit are quite acceptable as everyone knows the rules.

2 The idealist, who believes in total honesty and transparency at every step of a negotiation.

3 The pragmatist, who lies somewhere in the middle, trusting that what goes around comes around, whether legal deceit or honesty.

By the time you start work, the kind of negotiator you are will be already fixed, and if you try to change, or find yourself in situations where you are forced to, it will be profoundly uncomfortable.

Our basic sense of ethics is one of the hardest things to change. Consequently, if you feel squeamish about the idea of negotiating as a game, then you should try to seek out a role or business in which long-term relationships matter, in which each side must live with the consequences of a negotiation. If you are happy to think of negotiating as poker, then highly transactional businesses where you never see the other party again, may be for you. But if you feel you are sinking to the other party's standards, assert your position, and if it isn't going to be accepted, get out while you can.

There are also three types of information in a negotiation:

1 The basic substance of the negotiation, the numbers, the costs, the revenues and strategic implications. But if you stop there, you are missing what really matters.

2 The beliefs and feelings between the parties, their relations with each other. Challenged to negotiate sharing an identical set of assets, a divorcing couple might have a very different negotiation from two sympathetic and understanding business partners.

3 The process of a negotiation. Do you conduct it in a cold room, early in the morning, or in armchairs late at night, a glass of whisky in your hand? Do you press for a decision, or try to drag out the talks forever? Whom do you allow in the room? All the lawyers and accountants and colleagues? Or do you prefer to go one on one?[9]

The great negotiator understands all of these, in the way a musician knows scales and chords, and can then improvise depending on the circumstances, persuading, collaborating, haggling or bullying as required.

After all, no negotiation is conducted purely at the table. Rarely is it just about the deal in question. It often involves an array of external factors, such as the desire for power, or the fear of losing, a sense of embarrassment or triumph. The numbers will be just one piece of this. The rest is how people feel.

Understanding the substance of a negotiation and the opportunity to create shared value, rather than carve out more of the existing pie for yourself, should drive a powerful inter-personal process. Rarely do negotiations mark the beginning and end of a relationship between two parties. More often, they will be negotiating again and again over time. Make sure you consider this in each negotiation. Pressing too hard or giving in today may have good or bad consequences in the next round of negotiation or the one after that.

---

[9] 'Planning to Play it by Ear', Kathleen L. McGinn, *Harvard Business Publishing Newsletters*, 2003

Discovering what the other person really wants – and often money or titles are just a piece of it – then finding a way to deliver it is the key to a successful negotiation. Employees who dislike their job may actually only dislike their hours and how it takes them away from their family. A good manager should be able to find a solution, such as letting them work fewer hours for lower pay.

> discovering what the other person wants and finding a way to deliver it is the key to successful negotiation

Differences in tax and accounting can offer other ways to create value in a negotiation, as can disagreements over forecasts, cost and revenue structures or pricing of risk. An investment that only makes sense for one investor when it yields 10 per cent may be profitable for another at just 7 per cent. One company may have tax credits which another does not, and these can be used in a discussion over price.

Mastery at negotiation takes an enormous amount of practice. Managers can begin by opening their minds to all the possibilities a good negotiation presents.

Then familiarise yourself with the many tactics a good negotiator can use. Only experience will teach you when and how to deploy them, when to bluff, when to threaten, when to use deadlines and delays, or when to log-roll, a tactic of making a big deal of conceding on small items in order to get what you really want. But the better you get at each of these, the more you will find that negotiating, done well, can be one of the most enjoyable aspects of management.

Fostering innovation[10]

Bob Iannucci, the former chief technology officer at Nokia, used to give a talk about the evolutionary patterns in the technology

---

[10] Parts of this section are taken from Delves Broughton, P., 'A new route from idea to reality', *The Financial Times*, 3 November 2010. © The Financial Times Limited 2010. All rights reserved. For the full article, see the appendix at the back of the book.

industry called 'I've seen this movie before'. In it he described how every big technological change, from mainframes to minicomputers to PCs, had followed the same path. PCs, for example, began with several companies – Apple, Commodore, Wang and others – offering their own incompatible hardware and software. Then a standard platform emerged in IBM. Compatible hardware followed – Dell, Hewlett-Packard, Intel and Compaq – before the value shifted to software – Microsoft – and finally to services and companies such as IBM, EDS and Oracle.

By 2011, the same pattern appeared to be unfolding again in mobile phone technology. First, we had an array of separate systems, from Microsoft to Nokia, before a platform war emerged, waged most aggressively by Google's Android and Apple's iPhone operating systems. Hardware makers and the developers of software and mobile services were all circling this piranha tank, trying to decide which platform would thrive or die, and which to invest in.

The difference between the history of mobile technology and that of PCs is the pace of the change. Product development cycles are now faster than traditional corporate innovation structures seem able to cope with. And while some, such as Apple and Google, have seemed comfortable with the speed of change, others such as Nokia and RIM have been criticised for playing innovation catch-up with the Silicon Valley swells.

Every manager can learn from watching these battles unfold about how to keep innovation alive under the intense pressure of day-to-day competition.

The challenge in these innovation wars is not finding opportunity or the right technology. It is making sense of them all and coalescing them into a vision. It is giving meaning to this abundance of ideas and making it useful to consumers. In 2009, as a percentage of revenue, Nokia spent four times as much as Apple on research and development last year, and yet it had no market-changing products to show for it. Apple, meanwhile, surged ahead with its iPhones and plans for the iPad.

What made the difference? A key part of it was that Apple made their technology meaningful, while Nokia did not. Features and performance are not goods in themselves. They only matter if they do something useful for the customer. What excites an internal research group may fall flat in the market.

what excites an internal research group may fall flat in the market

When RIM came up with the BlackBerry, it perceived that what many users most wanted from their phones was email, and they could happily do without the rest of the operating software. Apple was not the first to make an MP3 player, but the good-looking iPod combined with iTunes removed the whiff of illegality around music downloads. Apple was similarly the first to make sense of touchscreen technology with its iPhone. It was more than a gimmick: it changed how people thought of their phones.

Apple's edge arose from Steve Jobs's experience in the entertainment industry. As the founder of Pixar, when he returned to Apple in 1996 he came at the music, movie and gaming industries as an insider. By being able to interpret the world beyond computers, he could arrange the puzzle of content and technology more successfully than most others. This proved a vital managerial skill.

Nokia tried to break its closed innovation loop by using ethnographers to observe how people use their mobile phones. In Africa they found people trading in calling card minutes, which could be redeemed for cash as a basic kind of banking. In India, they discovered servants were using their mobile phones to find new employers, thereby freeing them from indentured servitude. Such research helped Nokia think about innovative ways of serving huge numbers of customers in emerging markets. But as of 2011, it hadn't helped the company's profits.

Eric von Hippel, professor of technological innovation at the MIT Sloan School of Management, says a technology company should divide its research and innovation tasks 'into those it can solve internally and those that can most effectively be solved outside'. The ones that can be solved within are 'dimension-of-merit' improvements such as better screen resolution, ergonomics or interface design. Those that must be solved outside are those that involve new customer needs.

In 2007, for example, when Apple first released the iPhone, thousands of users decided to 'jail-break' the software in order to customise it. Prof. von Hippel says this prompted Steve Jobs to release a software developer kit, which in turn led to the explosion of the App Store. Apple was forced by outside events to open up its platform, although it remains controlled. 'Senior managers have to recognize that the innovation system has to be fundamentally reworked', says Prof. von Hippel. 'It's not a matter of tweaking. There is a fundamental new paradigm out there.' This new model was created by falling design and communication costs, which have enabled more people to be part of the process.

Prof. von Hippel says managers need to venture out to the leading edges of their market and engage with users. He calls it 'democratizing innovation'.

A similar view, espoused by Professor Roberto Verganti of the Politecnico di Milano, is that managers must listen to 'interpreters' – individuals inside and outside the company capable of understanding cultural and social forces beyond their immediate worlds. These are not traditional market researchers, but people from other industries and professions who look at what you are doing with fresh eyes.

Not every manager can afford to hire cultural anthropologists. But anyone can take a moment to look at their organisation and products as an outsider, or ask friends and family what they think, and try to link what they do to the broader culture.

When Jobs returned to Apple in 1997, he did not decide to be a technological leader, though Apple's software and hardware are in certain aspects innovative. He chose to take existing technologies and be innovative about packaging them up and creating a seamlessly integrated network around them which could enhance a consumer's life.

It may seem startling that such an idea could be so effective, but Apple's remarkable recovery, to the point where it became the world's most valuable technology company, is testament to this managerial approach.

Creating a networked environment

Technology has given us the false impression that all communication can be done via telephones, email and videoconferences. It is not true. It matters to see people in the flesh, even if you are managing them remotely. It is even more important when you are managing a complex process which relies on creativity and interaction.

In 1986, BMW set up its Group Research and Innovation Centre, known by its German acronym, FIZ. It occupies a set of buildings called the Projekthaus, where BMW comes up with designs for its cars. It was built to encourage 'process-oriented thinking'. In practice this means several things. The main rooms were made as large and adaptable as gymnasiums. Leading off them were smaller 'caves' for specialists to meet and share computerised or clay models. Then there is an atrium, flooded with natural light, where people cross paths endlessly.

The central idea behind the Projekthaus is that physical proximity and face-to-face meetings trump even the most sophisticated technology when it comes to dreaming up and implementing ideas.

It used to be that cars were designed in a series of consecutive steps. Not any more. BMW practises a process called 'simultaneous engineering' in which components are designed simultaneously. The architecture of the Projekthaus includes short walking routes between different locations so that people can find each other and the information they need as easily as possible. They can just get up and walk.

This is about much more than making car designers feel pampered. It boils down to the changing nature of customer desire. With so many cars on the market, and with technology changing so rapidly, car companies cannot afford to just design and launch a single product and hope for the best. Customers demand customisation. They want features which speak to them. They want sustainability and efficiency, luxury and safety, speed and economy. To deliver all of this, BMW needed a production system as versatile as their customers' imaginations. They needed to create a mass production system which created personalised cars.

This meant encouraging designers to experiment with new concepts and materials for cars years before they might go into production. 'It is in the nature of such visions that they do not necessarily claim to be suitable for series production', the company said. 'Rather they are intended to steer creativity and research into new directions. This approach helps to tap into formerly inconceivable, innovative potential that reaches far beyond the appearance of future cars and takes into account not only materials and structures but also functions and manufacturing processes. The potential requirements of tomorrow's customers serve as a benchmark.'

By allowing such visions to be developed in the heart of its organisation, BMW hoped to spawn innovative manufacturing concepts which would inspire industry-leading manufacturing. Once it could imagine the cars of the future, it could refine an interdisciplinary, rapid-manufacturing approach to create these highly customised components within a mass-production process. Such integrated management is far from easy. But it begins with managers thinking about a process for innovation which can then affect the culture and habits of their entire organisation.

For BMW, changing how cars were designed meant changing how the entire organisation was designed, down to the flow of people through its buildings. It offers two vital lessons to every manager. First, that any change must be thought through in the broadest possible terms if it is to have the desired effect. Second, that it is really important to recognise the limits of technology in allowing the deepest and most creative human relationships to flourish.

Top 10 tips for managing processes

1   Focus on process improvement as a means to creativity and innovation.

2   Pay attention to every step of your processes. None are too small.

3   Think and then explain your thinking in as clear a way as you know how. Don't hide behind PowerPoint.

4   Don't waste other people's time with meetings they don't need to attend.

5   Divide meetings into process meetings, such as monthly reviews, and decision meetings, those called ad hoc to reach a decision. Process meetings will be more formal, while decision meetings can be much more flexible in terms of format, guest list and style.

6   Escape the tyranny of the clock. If a meeting does not need to run on for the scheduled hour, cut it short.

7   Consider who you are negotiating with, not just what you are negotiating about.

8   Environment matters as much to process as the process itself. A well-designed office, or well-structured meetings and workflows are vital to a healthy business.

9   Divide your processes into those best done inside your company and those best done outside. Devote your resources only to those you do best.

10 When starting a new process, stay lean as long as possible in order to stay adaptable while you figure out what exactly it is you are doing.

Chapter 4

Managing numbers

What topics are covered in this chapter?

- Prioritising profit
- Breaking the link between strategic planning and budgeting
- Measuring performance
- Managing risk
- Interpreting numerical data

A manager needs to understand enough about finance and accounting to ensure two things: profitability and sound risk management. The rest, from earnings per share to the latest regulatory ruling, are for others to worry about. If a manager can get a firm hold on free cash flow and how to control it, he will be streets ahead of his rivals.

It is all too easy for companies to lose sight of their need to make a profit. When a company starts out, cash flow is foremost in everyone's mind. But as the company grows and the sources of financing multiply, products and services proliferate and divisions and new territories spring up, the focus on profit can become blurred. Accounting gimmicks can creep in, people start to play commission systems, and you end up with everyone in the company claiming they are generating profits, and yet the company as a whole is staring at a loss.

In almost every company, 20 to 30 per cent of the business is highly profitable, and those profits are used to subsidise the unprofitable parts. Most existing management systems do not help identify which are which, nor help turn those unprofitable parts around.

For many companies dealing with losses or declining profitability, the first reaction is to reassess strategy. A better starting point might be taking a hard look at the efficiency of their existing operations, to get right down to the invoice level and find out what money is coming in and how it is being spent.

Managers who get into the numbers at this level of granularity have a much better chance of finding out what is really going on, office by office, product by product and customer by customer, before the accounts get rolled up into the kind of neat, company-wide spreadsheets presented to senior executives. Very often they will find that all is not what it seems. All products and customers, after all, are not equal. There will be customers who place large orders but demand repeated deliveries rather than single, bulk drop-off. There will be products deemed 'strategic' which appear to have high margins, but demand so much customisation they end up losing money.

The trick here, as with so much in management, is clearing the undergrowth so you can see the truth, to discern which of your activities, products and customers are profitable first individually, and only then as a group. Only once you have a clear map of where your profits lie and a sense of what you can do to maximise them can you then set about trying to increase them. Otherwise you may as well be the subject of that old joke, when one man says to another 'you're losing money on every sale', and the other replies, 'yes, but we'll make it up on volume'.

Marketing experts love to talk about the four Ps of product, place, promotion and price, but a fifth also needs to be added: profit-ability. Without that, all the rest are worthless.[1]

Profitability is the responsibility of every manager, from the CEO to the department head to the front-line manager. This is even more relevant today as fewer products target mass markets, and more seek out ever finer niches. There is no longer one kind of spaghetti sauce, but dozens catering to every taste. Once basic products like denim jeans now come in myriad forms, fashions and price ranges. To manage such diversity, managers need to keep an

---

[1] *Islands of Profit in a Sea of Red Ink: Why 40% of your Business Is Unprofitable and How to Fix It*, Jonathan Byrnes, Viking, 2010

understanding of the profitability of each product and customer segment straight, by understanding account management, supply chains and the impact of relentless change.

This of course takes time, discipline and a willingness to make decisions based in uncertainty. If profitability were so easy to discern, there would be no advantage to the manager who goes searching for it. But it rarely is, so you will be rewarded if you are one of those who each month tries to drill down to the transaction level of your business to see what is really going on. You may only ever have incomplete information, but month after month, as you gather transaction data and piece it together with the rest of your company's operations, the closer you will come to grasping the truth. Repeat this cycle every year, wherever you may be in your career, and you will have information which even the most senior executives would covet.

As you consider products and customer accounts from a profit-ability perspective, you can then make decisions based on some very simple questions:

- Which are the most profitable?
- Are there more products like these out there, or customers willing to buy them?
- Can we increase the profits of any of them?
- And if their profits can't be increased, should we get rid of them altogether?

Even companies with excellent profits today will battle to sustain them. Researchers have found again and again that outsized returns on equity tend to revert to the norm over 10 to 15 years.[2] Companies whose returns on equity beat the S&P handsomely one year, will be back fighting it out with the pack ten years later.

---

[2] *Financial Strategy: Studies in the Creation, Transfer and Destruction of Shareholder Value*, William E. Fruhan, The Free Press, 1991

Firms such as Coca-Cola, Microsoft and Wal-Mart, which beat this mediocrity trap and continue to deliver abnormal profits for more than 15 years are rare, and rightly held dear by their shareholders.

Finding value in what you know

Value is one of those terms better understood outside business than inside. Any household bill payer knows the difference between good and bad value. Most of us have a keen sense of whether goods are priced fairly or not. But step into the corporate world, and suddenly the term goes wobbly.

There is shareholder value, but also stakeholder value; there is not one bottom line but multiple ones; there is intangible value and the value of potential synergies, which bump up acquisition prices before frequently turning to dust. When the American investor Warren Buffett talks of 'value investing' he is talking about buying great companies at good prices, rather than investing on the basis of all the other mind-bending signals and stimuli in the markets.

What managers at every level need to do is block out the noise and return to a simpler, less confusing idea of value.

At its most basic, the value of a business is the sum of the present value of its future expected cash flows. But as anyone who has ever tried to build a discounted cash flow model can attest, bankers and corporate finance professors could dance on the head of this one intellectual pin for eternity. How do you price risk? Do different cash flows carry different levels of risk? How do you know what the future really holds?

So, managing for value has to mean something more specific. There are four basic facts a manager needs to understand about value:[3]

[3] *Value: The Four Cornerstones of Corporate Finance*, McKinsey & Company Inc., Tim Koller, Richard Dobbs and Bill Huyett, John Wiley & Sons, 2010

1   Companies create value by investing capital to generate future cash flows at higher rates of return than their cost of capital.

2   Companies create value by generating higher cash flows, not by rejigging the capital structure by cutting or increasing debt, or issuing or buying back stock.

3   Expectations drive a company's stock price as well as its actual performance, so the higher your expectations, the faster you must run to keep up.

4   The value of a business depends in large part on who is managing it and the strategy they pursue. A good owner or good manager can dramatically transform the value of a business.

Responsible investors are focused on long-term value, and it is with them that a good manager should wish to be aligned. They do not twitch in response to every crumb of news flashing by on their Bloomberg Terminal. Instead, they think about value in terms of its four basic elements. Do we have the best managers and owners in place? Are they pursuing the right strategy? And are they producing returns that exceed our cost of capital and will they continue to do so? If so, over time the value of our investment will be properly priced, regardless of any fleeting swoons and spasms exhibited by the markets.

A manager whose performance is being measured by his company's share price needs to know what makes that share price move and whether it is a fair measure.

Case Study

In 2010, Peter Löscher, the chief executive of Siemens, announced that after ten years of managerial effort invested in turning the company around, it was time to start performing again. After a decade in which Siemens's share price barely moved, investors suddenly bubbled with expectation and the ▶

company's share price rose accordingly. Mr Löscher and his predecessors were not rewarded by the markets while their overhaul of the company was going on. It only happened once Siemens was fixed and ready to grow. Recognition of value is not a linear process. The manager sees it one day, everyone else the next, which explains why share prices often move in spurts, upwards or downwards based on events, rather than more steadily in line with the facts.

Misunderstanding value can lead to several bad outcomes. The first is plain recklessness. Companies with excellent returns in one area often fritter them away in another. When executives have their compensation linked to the size of their company, directly or indirectly, they are tempted to make poor acquisitions or invest in projects with negative net present value. Warren Buffett, described this phenomenon in his 1984 letter to investors:

> *Many corporations that show consistently good returns have, indeed, employed a large portion of their retained earnings on an economically unattractive, even disastrous, basis. Their marvelous core businesses camouflage repeated failures in capital allocation elsewhere (usually involving high-priced acquisitions). The managers at fault periodically report on the lessons they have learned from the latest disappointment. They then usually seek out future lessons. (Failure seems to go to their heads.) . . . In such cases, shareholders would be far better off if the earnings were retained to expand only the high-return business, with the balance being paid in dividends or used to repurchase stock.*

The opposite danger is that fear of negative returns drives managers to become recklessly cautious. They become so focused on today's earnings per share, and frozen by the fear of punishment by the stock market if that number drops, they pass up terrific opportunities to create long-term value. It is not just individual managers and companies that suffer when this condition takes hold, but entire economies hankering for growth.

When managers understand value properly, however, the results can be spectacular.

In 2001, General Mills bought Pillsbury from Diageo for $10.4 billion. Diageo's main business was alcoholic drinks, whereas General Mills, like Pillsbury, sold packaged foods. Diageo did the right thing for its own business by operating Pillsbury as a separate organisation. When General Mills bought Pillsbury, it was able easily to find overlaps with Pillsbury's purchasing, manufacturing and distribution, and was able to push Pillsbury's products through its existing sales channels, notably into American schools.

Within a short time, Pillsbury's pre-tax cash flows had risen by over $400 million and its operating profits rose by 70 per cent. Pillsbury was worth more under General Mills than it was under Diageo. The owner best able to maximise the value of an individual company not only has distinctive management skills, but also has unique links with other businesses, across the value chain, from R&D and manufacturing to distribution and sales. Developing and marketing brands is the rare skill possessed by Procter & Gamble. It is capable of taking old brands, like Tide detergent and newer acquisitions like Gillette, and even internal start-ups, and imposing the same brand-building discipline on all of them before shunting them through their well-developed sales channels. Procter & Gamble does what it knows again and again, getting better each time. It increases its value by building on its existing strengths.

Case Study

During the 1990s, Intuit was making software for individuals to manage their personal finances when it noticed many small businesses were using their products. Its managers realised that most business accounting software was too complex for small business owners and so developed Intuit's own small ▶

business software, and within two years had 80 per cent of the market. In the mid-1980s, Williams Companies, an oil and natural gas company, realised that it could install fibre-optic cable into its decommissioned pipelines at lower cost than its competitors. It eventually controlled 11,000 miles of cable across the United States. It sold this business at a time when such assets were inflated in price, in 1994, for $25 billion. These are examples of managers discovering and unlocking value which might otherwise have passed unseen.

Critics of the private equity industry say that its successes depend solely on financial leverage. Cheap debt and a booming economy mean investors can buy companies with other people's money, make them more efficient and profitable and flip them on in a few years at a huge profit.

What these critics miss, however, is the vital role of good management in private equity. When companies are taken private and no longer have to fret about the reaction of the markets, they can focus on what really matters. Studies of private equity companies have shown that their board members spent three times as many days in these roles than their peers at public companies. And while at work, they spend most of their time on strategy and performance rather than compliance or risk avoidance, the dominant topic at public board meetings. Public boards tend to focus on control, short-term profits and meeting investor expectations. Private boards are more concerned with creating value over the long term rather than over the next quarter.[4]

If creating value depends on doing what you know, then this also means management has to change to keep up with changes to a company or its environment.

---

[4] 'The Voice of Experience: Public versus Private Equity', Viral Acharya, Conor Kehoe and Michael Reyner, *McKinsey on Finance*, Spring 2009, 16–21

It used to be the case, for example, that chemical and pharmaceutical companies formed a single unit. Zeneca was part of ICI. Aventis was part of Hoechst. But over time it became clear that the two businesses had very different management needs. Chemicals companies are commodity businesses, requiring scale, operating efficiency and tight cost management. Pharmaceutical companies must focus on R&D, regulation, sales forces and government relations. Once this became clear, Zeneca left ICI in 1993 and Aventis left Hoechst in 1999. Selling a business or changing its management is not an admission of failure, but rather a recognition of value.

Only managers at the very top of a company will get to buy and sell divisions. But every manager needs to understand which operations are profitable and what leads to those profits. You need to understand the financial value of what you do to your own company, so you can work to sustain and improve it, and what it might be worth to others, so you can manage your own career.

Managing for value

How do you deliver near-term profits while investing for the long term? This is one of the greatest and most enduring challenges for managers, this balance between keeping investors and employees happy now while finding the time and resources to plan for the future. The more complex a business, the more it tends to focus on short-term earnings, as those are the most visible measure. Growing earnings faster than revenues is a laudable short-term goal. But there may be severe long-term implications to cutting costs, or failing to invest.

> the more complex a business, the more it tends to focus on short-term earnings

In one notable survey, 400 chief financial officers were asked about what they would do to meet their quarterly earnings target:

80 per cent said they were willing to cut discretionary expenditures in marketing and product development even at the cost of long-term performance; 55 per cent said they would delay value-creating projects if they reduced short-term earnings.[5]

It's not easy overcoming short-term bias. People are always there to criticise and it's hard to convince them of the benefits of cutting present returns in favour of future ones.

One place to start when trying to resolve this problem is with compensation. Executives who are rewarded based on hitting quarterly earnings benchmarks will be motivated to value the short over the long term. Any compensation plan needs to tie short- and long-term performance together and requires more than a purely mechanical approach. Executives should be rewarded based on both earnings per share and share price and other factors such as product development, employee development and customer satisfaction. Share prices, after all, can be affected as much in the short term by expectations as by actual performance. The last thing you want to do as a manager is to help raise your company share price by increasing expectations and then failing to deliver.

Similarly, any important managerial discussions, from strategy and planning to board meetings, need to focus on this issue in detail. What are the trade-offs to be made? An open discussion early in the planning and review processes will make any subsequent decisions much easier.

Breaking the links between strategic planning and budgeting is a good place to start. Strategic planning should operate under a different timeline to budget planning, so strategy does not emerge simply as a five-year budget plan. It should focus on long-term creators of value for the entire organisation, and be distinct from business unit strategy. It should ask questions such as what

[5] 'Value Destruction and Financial Reporting Decisions', John Graham, Cam Harvey and Shiva Rajgopal, *Financial Analysts Journal*, 62, 2006

businesses should we exit or develop, not simply how much everything costs.

When you do get to budgeting, avoid any approach which regards all operations as uniform. Ordering cuts of five per cent across the board suggests that every part of your business is the same, which makes no sense.

Ideally, managers should understand the trade-offs between long-term and short-term performance, strategy and opportunity at their own business level.

In discussing financial performance, it's far better to focus on your return on invested capital and revenue growth, which are relatively clean numbers, than accounting profits or profit growth, which can conceal all manner of corporate filth. But these are still backward-looking measures. You can have a division which is increasing returns and profits for years by cutting forward-looking expenditures like marketing, until one day it simply collapses. It's like removing spokes one by one from a bicycle wheel. It will be fine for a while, until one day the bike gives way under you. If all you do is keep cutting costs or raising prices to increase short-term profit, with no regard for the future, you will eventually hit a point where you cannot raise prices any more and your market share starts to fall, and you are stuck. It takes years to recover from this, to regain that lost position. Avoid such steroid-fuelled growth and focus instead on healthy living.

Good performance measurement can help overcome the short-term bias of financial measures. It will tell you how well your business is positioned to both maintain and improve its perform-ance, or general good health. These measures can be broken down into short-term value drivers, such as sales productivity, operating cost productivity and capital productivity; medium-term drivers, such as general commercial health, the sustainability of your growth, product pipeline, brand and customer base, cost structure, how you match up to competitors in the coming years, and asset health, how you maintain and improve your assets' productivity over time. Anyone who stays frequently in hotels can tell the difference between a chain with healthy assets and one which skimps on refreshing its rooms. Then finally there are long-term value drivers, such as strategic exploitation of new growth ventures, investments in people's skills, and developing healthy flows of talent and R&D.

It is the manager's duty to ensure that no one in the organisation is oblivious to the fact of these trade-offs and how they apply to their own job, even if they do not understand all of the specifics.

Ignoring the facts[6]

Ideally, your decisions should be based on sound evidence. But often, managers make a decision then rustle up the evidence to support it. As Peter Tingling and Michael Brydon of Simon Fraser University have written, it is the difference between evidence-based decision making and its ugly sibling, decision-based evidence making.[7]

At the Battle of Copenhagen, Lord Nelson was told that his commander was signalling for him to retreat, Nelson raised a telescope to his blind eye and said: 'I really do not see the signal.' Within a few hours, the Danish fleet was defeated, with Nelson the hero. He had made the decision to fight and moulded the evidence to fit. The successful outcome justified his decision.

But in a world that venerates data-driven decision making, whether in financial services or sports management, managers are often loath to admit that they still take the Nelson approach to make

---

[6] Parts of this section are taken from Delves Broughton, P. 'When to turn a blind eye to the facts', *The Financial Times*, 20 September 2010. © The Financial Times Limited 2010. All rights reserved. For the full article, see the appendix at the back of the book.

[7] 'Is Decision-based Evidence Making Necessarily Bad?', Peter Tingling and Michael Brydon, *MIT Sloan Management Review*, June 2010

the decision first and find the evidence later.

> managers are often loath to admit that they ... make the decision first and find the evidence later

Professors Tingling and Brydon found that evidence is used by managers in three different ways: to make, inform or support a decision. If it is used to make a decision, it means the decision arises directly from the evidence. If it is used to inform a decision, evidence is mixed in with intuition or bargaining to lead to a decision. If it is used to support a decision, it means the evidence is simply a means to justify a decision already made. They also found that evidence is often shaped by subordinates to meet what they perceive to be the expectations of their bosses.

There are two dangers to letting decisions trump evidence:

1 When decision making is simply ill-informed. Ideally, a decision that contradicts the evidence is an inspired hunch, formed by experience, like Nelson's. In the worst case, it is the product of ignorant bias.

2 Once your employees know that you, as a manager, are more interested in finding evidence to fit your conclusions rather than seeking out truth, it infects a company with demoralising and destructive cynicism.

When Herman Miller designed the Aeron chair, consumer focus groups were hostile. But the company ignored them and went ahead with production anyway. The chair was a huge hit. The company was capable of taking evidence and successfully ignoring it.

In other companies, however, the cult of data-driven decision making leaves so little room for personal beliefs that people just tailor evidence to fit pre-made decisions.

At Ford in the 1950s, Robert McNamara, then chief executive, demanded data on everything. Interns would cut up newspapers and paste them into binders so executives could point to the voluminous research that went into each decision.

Vince Kaminski, who led Enron's research division, has spoken of the frustrations of having 50 highly skilled mathematicians picking apart Enron's risky deals only to be ignored by executives who prized trading volume and revenue growth above all else.

So what is a manager to do? How do you encourage the use of data, while leaving room for the occasional inspired decision? One solution is to be more flexible in how you categorise decisions. Not all will require the same degree of evidence.

Another is to weigh the costs of gathering evidence. Is it always worth it? If not, don't fudge it for appearance's sake. Admit that you are trusting your well-honed instincts. This is especially true for those within your company. Sometimes you will have to come up with tendentious evidence for an external audience, which demands at least a charade of evidence. But don't ever pretend for those inside. They will know better and punish the slightest deceit either now or well into the future.

Managing risk

Cash flow is at the heart of risk management. If a company can generate sufficient internal cash flow it can fund value-enhancing investments. If it has to go outside for the money by issuing debt or equity, its behaviours change. It can become either too cautious, if the money comes with too many strings attached, or too reckless, if the consequences of spending it fall solely on the investors.

Existing shareholders fret if a company dilutes their equity in a new fundraising. And raising debt involves discussions with banks, modified interest rates and all manner of legal provisions. It explains why companies which do not generate enough cash internally tend to cut too far in vital areas, thereby stunting their growth. One study in America found that companies cut their

capital expenditures by 35 cents for every dollar lost in cash flow.[8]
Even when a great investment opportunity comes along, those who cannot self-finance would rather let it go by than go through the hassle of reaching outside for the cash.

> companies which do not generate enough cash internally tend to cut too far in vital areas

Cash is also the greatest shield against factors beyond the manager's control, from currency movements and interest rates to the price of inputs, whether commodities or labour. With cash, a company can continue to invest, whatever the macro conditions.

The purpose of risk management then is to ensure a company can continue to make investments which increase its value. You always want enough cash on hand to boost value.

The first instance of a financial option appears in the writings of Aristotle. Thales the Milesian, a philosopher, predicted from a reading of tea leaves that in six months' time there would be an unusually abundant olive harvest. With what little money he had, he went to the owners of some local oil presses and bought the right to rent them at the usual rate during the harvest season. Sure enough, the harvest was abundant and growers were desperate for access to the presses. Thales exercised his rental right for the normal rate and then sold it on for a much higher rate, pocketing the difference.

Company managers today follow Thales' example in all kinds of ways. Oil producers may seek to sell the right to buy their output at a fixed price today if they believe prices will fall in the future. Farmers may strike a deal to pay a certain amount for feed throughout the winter, to protect themselves from fluctuating prices. Options and hedging provide managers with a new set of

---

[8] 'Financing Constraints and Corporate Investments', Steven Fazzari, R. Glenn Hubbard and Bruce Petersen, *Brookings Papers on Economic Activity*, no. 1, 1988, p. 141

tools to achieve their core purpose of matching their company's supply of funds with demands for those funds. For example, if you are managing a plant in Italy which makes products for the UK market, you may want to keep a close eye on the euro/sterling exchange rate and hedge accordingly. If the euro appreciates and you are still selling your products for sterling, your profit margins will decrease. But on the other hand, the value of investing in your Italian plant decreases, so you have less need for euro funds. The key point to bear in mind is not just how much cash you are generating, but what you need that cash for.

It may be tempting for a manager to wash his hands of all this and leave it up to the finance division. But that would be a grievous mistake. The finance department only exists to ensure that managers have cash to make value-enhancing investments. If a financial decision inhibits that ability, then it is your duty as a manager to complain.

If an opportunity comes up and you are unable to pay for it, whether it is an employee that needs to be hired or a plant which needs upgrading, or a start-up that should be acquired, then finance has created a managerial problem which the manager must demand be solved. Managers need to understand enough about the financial decision-making process at their companies to be able to make the case for spending where necessary and to understand when cuts need to be made.

Focusing on relevance rather than rules

Accounting is about information, not about the rules or arcane practices of accountants. It involves measurement, interpretation and judgement, which makes it as much art as science, more like the law than mathematics. Accounts can be fudged, massaged or even used as tools of outright deceit. There will be one set for the auditors and tax authorities, and another for managers to use to conduct their operations.

When compiling or reading accounts, a manager has to consider what in them is relevant, and what reliable. Often they will contain numbers and metrics which are neither. Managers must be alert to the inevitability of bias and measurement error and weigh them against their own view of economic reality.

A surge in sales one quarter may be the result of an unusual compensation plan which leads to a slump the next. Cash flow and net income may be different numbers depending on factors ranging from depreciation schedules to deferred tax payments. The physical flow of goods in and out of a warehouse, and how you value them, may be handled differently by warehouse managers and tax accountants. Healthy cash flow is what keeps a business open and to understand it properly you need to go further than the numbers on a spreadsheet.

Cash can come in one month and be recorded as income long before a service is delivered. The inflows and outflows of cash do not always correspond with the products or services provided or the costs incurred.

> cash can come in one month and be recorded as income long before a service is delivered

But it is not just finances which can be usefully accounted for.

In 1992, Robert Kaplan and David Norton presented the idea of a Balanced Scorecard, a way for companies to improve the measurement and management of their intangible assets. They were inspired by the words of the British scientist Lord Kelvin: 'When you can measure what you are speaking about, and express it in numbers, you know something about it; but when you cannot measure it, when you cannot express it in numbers, your knowledge is of a meagre and unsatisfactory kind. If you can not measure it, you can not improve it.'[9]

[9] Sir William Thompson (Baron Kelvin of Largs), Lecture on 'Electrical Units of Measurement' (delivered 1883), *Popular Lectures and Addresses, Volume 1*, Macmillan, 1889, pp. 73–4

They argued that while financial metrics remained the final measure of a company's success, in order to understand how you create long-term shareholder value, managers needed also to measure progress along three other dimensions: customers; internal processes; and learning and growth. This helps avoid the short-term bias discussed above.

The Balanced Scorecard was inspired by a 1950s effort at General Electric to measure divisional performance by one financial and seven non-financial metrics. These were:

1 Profitability

2 Market share

3 Productivity

4 Product leadership

5 Public responsibility – to the law, ethics, shareholders, vendors, distributors and communities

6 Personnel development

7 Employee attitudes

8 The balance between short- and long-term objectives.

This eighth and final metric encapsulated the spirit of the Balanced Scorecard and is at the heart of good management. Any fool can jack up short-term profitability by sacrificing long-term success. Similarly, the business world is full of people who make their living talking about five- and ten-year plans with no regard for this year's performance. The great manager finds a way to navigate between these two extremes, to satisfy the need to do well today, this quarter, while developing his organisation for the future. It is an immensely difficult task. Despite GE's best efforts, several of its units were later convicted of price-fixing, and its managers blamed the company's focus on short-term profits over long-term growth and public responsibility.[10]

---

[10] 'Conceptual Foundations of the Balanced Scorecard', *Working Paper 10–074*, HBSP, Robert S. Kaplan, 2010

It is very hard in certain cultures for managers to escape the focus on short-term financial performance. Magazine covers and investors venerate CEOs who provide steady upward growth in earnings. Far less visible or valued are investments in long-term employee development. In fact, many companies far prefer to invest in tangible assets, such as physical products or plant, or even acquisitions, than in intangible assets such as employee skills, process innovation or customer satisfaction. The Balanced Scorecard was an effort to deliver meaningful metrics on the performance and management of these intangible assets so they could receive the attention they deserved.

Unlike a factory, intangible assets are all but worthless on their own. They take on value dependent on their context and how they are bundled with other assets. A wildly creative graphic designer may be useless if told to improve the look of a stodgy corporate brochure, but brilliant when asked to overhaul all the visual tools of an international sportswear company. A great corporate lawyer, skilled in shipping negotiations, may botch a simple house purchase. To measure their talents or potential out of context would be meaningless. But measuring them in context is difficult because of the complex web of causes and effects which lead to their success.

Similarly, it is not always easy to make the links between, say, the effectiveness of a sales call, which may lead to greater customer satisfaction, which leads to greater loyalty, more sales and higher profitability. It takes work to sift through these links and make sense of them, to tie financial performance back to actions and processes deep inside your organisation. Financial economists have argued that by the simple measure of tying pay to perform-ance, you force managers to focus on all that makes a company work. But the inventors of the Balanced Scorecard were sceptical and argued for a more subtle, weighted measurement system.

'Consider an airplane where passengers contract with the pilot for a safe and on-time journey', wrote Kaplan. 'One can imagine an airplane cockpit designed by a financial economist. It consists of a single instrument that displays the destination to be achieved and the desired time of arrival. Or, the pilot is given a more complex navigation instrument where the movement of the needle represented a weighted average of estimated time to arrival, fuel remaining, altitude, deviation from expected flight path, and proximity to other airplanes. Few of us would feel comfortable flying in a plane guided only by the single instrument even though the incentives of the pilot and the passengers for a safe, on-time arrival are perfectly aligned. Incentives are important, but so also are information, communication, and alignment.'

The Balanced Scorecard sought to reconcile the frequent contradictions in management between complexity and focus. It tried to give managers a sound grasp of the many factors affecting performance while keeping their eye on the only one that ultimately matters: making consistent profits over time.

Its influence is now visible all over businesses and other forms of organisation. Harrah's, the data-obsessed casino and resort company, uses analytics to measure how its health and wellness programmes affect employee engagement. JetBlue created a score to measure their employees' willingness to recommend the company as a place to work, called the 'crewmember net promoter score'. This in turn helps measure the effect of changes to compensation. Highly satisfied employees, the company believes, lead to higher revenue.

Google has used a balanced scorecard-like measurement system to deduce that when hiring, a demonstrated ability to take initiative is a better predictor of success than a great academic record. The great Italian soccer club AC Milan compiles 60,000 data points on each of its players to assess their health and fitness, which helps them turn out better players and assess their market value much more precisely than if all they relied on was on-field performance.

At General Electric, a recent revolution in the marketing function has led to the chief marketing officers gathering their teams for an annual evaluation which measures performance in eight areas: strategy and innovation; branding and communications; sales force effectiveness; new world skills; market knowledge; segmentation and targeting; value creation and pricing; and commercial activation. These areas are then each broken down, to get to 35 skills with 140 definitions. For example, one of the skills of market knowledge is to identify external trends and influences. This skill has four definitions, ranging from understanding policy and regulation to social changes affecting customer need. Scores are issued for every definition and then rolled up into the eight categories. This creates benchmarks for improvement. It is hard work, but companies like GE find it is worth it for developing a proper grasp on their company's people and operations.

The Balanced Scorecard is ultimately about management not measurement. The metrics themselves are not important, especially if they simply multiply and become a problem in themselves. What matters is whether they lead to managers making better decisions. They should allow the manager to make better diagnoses which lead to better treatments. Their very existence should also lead to changed behaviours.

If people know they are being measured along these dimensions and that their scores will be used to evaluate them, their behaviour will adapt accordingly. They should also lead to richer discussions of particular problems. They direct the conversation towards action and solution. They become a management system which allows for the execution of corporate strategy.

Like any measurement system, the Balanced Scorecard depends ultimately on the involvement of leaders and managers. Only they determine what the scorecard will measure, what weights to give to each category and how they link back to strategy. Only they can decide how employees will use them to improve the business.

Managers and leaders are the only ones who can bring the sterile, random numbers to relevant life.

Top 10 tips for managing numbers

1 Find out what your company's cost of capital is and try to figure out if you and the people you manage provide a return which exceeds it.

2 Seek out relevance not rules in formal accounting.

3 Measure all you can, then decide afterwards if the measurement is meaningful and useful.

4 Focus on cash flow, not the formal profit and loss statement.

5 Don't be inhibited by arbitrary reporting periods of months, quarters or years. Your goal is long-term value.

6 Visit the finance department and ask how capital is allocated and how revenue and costs are accounted for at the corporate level.

7 Compare these allocations with those in your own unit. Any discrepancies may distort perceptions of your performance.

8 Use cash sparingly as a form of risk management. The more you have on hand, the more flexibility you will have when making decisions.

9 Share the numbers and how they were calculated with those you manage. Invite criticism. It helps depersonalise performance appraisals.

10 Use profitability targets to maintain focus on what really matters in your business.

Chapter 5
Managing yourself

What topics are covered in this chapter?

- The pros and cons of 'crisis-culture'
- Defining a vision for change
- Generating support
- Dodging common pitfalls
- Dealing with by-products of change

T he Harvard professor Michael Beer has proposed the following formula for understanding change in an organisation:

Amount of Change = (Dissatisfaction * Model * Process) > Cost of change

The idea is that for any change to happen, the people within an organisation must be so dissatisfied that the perceived rewards of overhauling their existing operating model and processes exceed the nuisance and anxiety of doing so. Dissatisfaction can take various forms, from a low-level boredom and a failure to attract interesting work or employees to an outright crisis, the so-called 'burning platform', when you are forced to change or else risk being immolated along with your business.

If your organisation needs to change, but there is no widespread dissatisfaction or sense of crisis, then it is up to the manager to engender one.

Samsung, the Korean electronics maker, has been called a 'perpetual crisis machine' because of its leadership's insistence that even a moment of relaxation could lead to disaster. In the men's toilets, there used to hang photographs of the planes striking the World Trade Center on 11 September 2001. The Korean caption explained that that disaster can strike from anywhere, so it is important to remain ever vigilant.

Yun Jong-Yong, who served as the company's CEO from 1996 to 2008 and turned Samsung into the most profitable electronics company in the world, told his employees that in the electronics business, the winners were first to market. Slow down for even a moment and your product would rapidly become a commodity and once that happens the lowest-cost manufacturers in China would take over your business. 'What makes a creature survive on earth is not its strength but its ability to adjust to a new environment', Yun liked to say.[1] This sense of impending doom extended even to the cafeteria, where toilet paper was used for napkins to save money.

> toilet paper was used for napkins to save money

When an American magazine asked one of Samsung's most senior engineers why he was willing to work 18–20 hours a day and forgo time with his young family, he said: 'I can say, "I drove down costs, created more value for the customer." Sure, maybe we work more than the normal eight hours, but because we do, the next generation may only have to work eight hours. We do it not only for our company and our families, but also for our country.'[2] Even at his peak as CEO, after leading Samsung to its dominant position in its industry, Jong-Yong Yun told the world, 'we stand at the crossroads to becoming a world leader or a major failure'. He was unapologetic about using this sense of fear to propel his company forward. 'You love your wife', he would say, 'but you still have to tell her that you love her every day.'

Samsung's crisis mentality may seem extreme, but it was forged in extreme circumstances. As late as the 1960s, South Korea was one of the poorest countries in the world, ravaged by Japanese occupation and then a ruinous civil war. It had none of the world-class industrial infrastructure and engineering expertise we see there today. Even as South Korea regained its footing, its entrepreneurs and managers were propelled by a profound need to prove themselves.

---

[1] 'Yun Jong-Yong Relishes Evolution', Choe Sang-Hun, *The New York Times*, 9 July 2005

[2] 'A Perpetual Crisis Machine', Peter Lewis, *Fortune*, 19 September 2005

In 1995, the company's then-chairman, Kun-Hee Lee, gave Samsung mobile phones to his friends and employees. To his profound embarrassment, the phones were riddled with glitches. So Lee ordered the entire inventory, some $50 million worth, to be placed in front of the factory where they were made and had the workers who had made them smash them up and burn them in front of Samsung's top managers. Thus began Samsung's final ascent, from commodity parts maker to global electronics brand. When Lee appointed Yun CEO in 1996, he recommended a unique strategy: 'Change everything except your spouse and children.' Yun was just starting to do so, when the 1997 Asian financial crisis forced Samsung to near bankruptcy. Yun wasted no more time, sacking a third of his employees, to the horror of those who had believed that in Korea a job was for life, and redirecting the company to focus on digital technologies.

Yun called his approach 'sincere management'. It required cutting costs to become competitive in the short term, then investing in research into vital technologies for the long haul. He believed that there was no point running a business which was no longer increasing its profits, nor entering a market in which Samsung could not be the market leader. To survive in the technology business, you had to adapt constantly and quickly, deliver quality and always be seeking out improvements to your processes, however minute.

For Yun, simply feeling dissatisfied was not enough. He ensured that everyone in his company shared his dissatisfaction, that everyone understood the competitive dynamics of their industry so that no one was confused over the need for paranoia. He also expected his managers to be the most dissatisfied people in his company, because they had spent the time uncovering areas for improvement throughout their organisation and desperately wanted to fix them.

Paranoia and constant dissatisfaction may sound like unpleasant features of a management system. But the reward of 'sincere management' and constantly being on your toes is a healthier company, more adaptive to sudden and frequent change.

Managers vs leaders

What is the difference between a manager and a leader? It is a question business academics adore, especially in discussions of managing change, but it has no real significance. In his classic article, 'Managers and Leaders: Are they Different?', Prof. Abraham Zaleznik described leaders as emotional, inspirational figures whose talents tended to be born rather than made. Managers, by contrast, were rational, practical, uncontroversial people who focused on getting things done. This is, of course, nonsense.

A great leader must also be a great manager of people and processes. Leadership is a subset of management, not a discipline apart. In business especially, a CEO who focuses solely on inspiration and emotion and ignores the practical aspects of management will very quickly be found out. The closer one looks at the great stories of business leadership, the more one realises that they are better understood as stories of effective management than of emotion or inspiration.

> leadership is a subset of management

One of the most famous corporate turnarounds was Lou Gerstner's management of IBM in the 1990s. Gerstner, a former management consultant at McKinsey and senior executive at American Express and RJR Nabisco, was hired to run IBM in 1993. His first day at work was April Fool's Day. When he arrived at the company, he found people speaking a company code, alien even to him, a business veteran. They talked of taking issues 'offline', of 'hard stops' and 'pushback', terms which may since have entered the business lexicon, but were novelties in 1993.

Absent from this code, Gerstner feared, was any kind of hard, cost-driven analysis. The problem with IBM was that it was living off the fat of a mighty past. It had been the greatest company in America at one time, a technological pioneer with fabled management and a legendary sales force, made up of its recognisable men in blue suits, white shirts and dark ties.

By the time Gerstner arrived, IBM still had 300,000 employees, but was losing billions of dollars. Worse, its lifelong managers seemed to have no idea what to do. Even a cursory glance at IBM's income statement told you here was a company with nothing left to lose. But to the thousands who came to work each day, trusting in IBM's history and culture, believing that Big Blue would take care of them for life, change seemed the most frightening thing of all.

'Transformation of an enterprise begins with a sense of crisis or urgency', Gerstner later recalled. 'No institution will go through fundamental change unless it believes it is in deep trouble and needs to do something different to survive.'[3]

Gerstner had the advantage of being an outsider. He would be allowed to do things no insider could. And fortunately, there were a few important people within the company who grasped the urgency of the situation and were willing to help. The first thing was to restore IBM to solvency, as it was close to running out of cash. Gerstner cut billions of dollars in expenses, laid off thousands of people, and sold assets to raise cash.

One might expect a former management consultant then to dig right into a strategic review. But Gerstner's view was that strategy wasn't going to pull IBM back from the brink. When a company is dying, it is more important to execute than strategise. 'You don't "win" with strategy', he said. 'Everybody's strategy in industry is fairly similar. There's no way to create a unique strategy. You can

---

[3] 'Gerstner – Changing Culture at IBM', *HBS Working Knowledge*, 9 December 2002

have a good one, but you can expect that your competitors are going to emulate it every day.'

The answer for IBM, Gerstner believed, was to revamp its processes and its culture to become what their customers needed, an integrator of a huge array of technologies, hardware and software, and services. He quickly put a stop to plans to break IBM up into different operating units. The company needed to be integrated within so that it could integrate on behalf of its customers.

'Internal integration' is a fancy term for getting people to work as a team. This was especially hard at IBM whose sales culture had long put tough, individualistic salespeople on a pedestal. Rather than being broken apart, IBM needed to be pulled together. The means of doing this lay in the details of the organisation.

Divisions within IBM needed to share their technical plans so that an integrated solution could be found for customers. Transfer pricing between products, which allowed each division to nibble away at each contract, was abolished. Systems across offices, territories and divisions were made uniform. Managers were stripped of their layers of assistants and subordinates and told to manage, not 'preside'.

Gerstner tied compensation to the performance of the whole company rather than a particular division, to try to stop employees competing against others within IBM. He required that each employee make three 'personal business commitments', which would lead to the fulfilment of IBM's larger goals. Compensation was linked directly to your performance against those commitments. He also urged employees to abandon the 'obsessive perfectionism' which gummed up IBM's operations, and emphasised the importance of getting work done well and fast, rather than perfectly every time. He abandoned pet technologies which had absorbed millions of dollars of investment with no return.

He fired many of the advertising agencies IBM was using, and handed the work to one, Ogilvy & Mather, instructing it to create a common brand for IBM's products and services around the world. He also ended the company's no-drinking policy and its mandatory dress code, allowing employees a little more slack to do what really mattered.

The hard process of re-engineering IBM to get it to focus on delivering value to customers, making it market-driven rather than simply satisfying the curious demands of its internal processes, provoked one senior IBM manager to rage: 'Reengineering is like starting a fire on your head and putting it out with a hammer.'

These managerial practices led to the unification of IBM's previously factional culture. Gerstner said of the importance of culture that 'It took me to age fifty-five to figure that out. I always viewed culture as one of those things you talked about, like marketing and advertising. It was one of the tools that a manager had at his or her disposal when you think about an enterprise. The thing I have learned at IBM is that culture is everything.'

Gerstner's achievement at IBM is studied today as an example of great leadership, but as he said, execution was everything at IBM. Management mattered. In his case, and most others, leadership and management are inextricably intertwined.

Observing unintended consequences of change

Organisations are not linear systems. Tinker with one aspect of them, and you might hope to cause a predictable effect in another part, but it does not always happen. Meteorologists have long been fascinated by the poetic sounding but profound question: does the flap of a butterfly's wings in Brazil set off a tornado in Texas? The idea is that even the slightest variation in an initial condition, as slight as the flap of a butterfly's wing, can dramatically transform an outcome.

Managers do not have time to focus so minutely on every aspect of what they and their organisation may do. But they should bear in mind right at the outset of any change effort that organisations consist of multiple interlocking parts, and that changing one is bound to lead to changes elsewhere. Tom Peters and Tony Athos developed their 7S framework to break the organisational model down into its hard elements, strategy, structure and systems, and soft elements, style, staff, skills and shared values.

Before introducing any change, managers must pull back from their business and see it in its entirety. Because once you start the process of change, you have to go all in if you want to keep people motivated to suffer through the inevitable discomfort.

If a manager understands the butterfly effect, he will be less surprised by all the twists and unforeseen consequences of the change process. By taking an integrated approach from the start, keeping his employees informed and encouraging them to participate, he will lower the risk of failure. There will always be resistance. Groups will emerge who do everything from gripe to launching outright challenges to your efforts. Some people will simply never accept that things must change. The only answer is to replace them as quickly as possible. While some people can be won around, others cannot and they are best ejected from the organisation promptly, before the toxicity of their opposition spreads.

> if a manager understands the butterfly effect, he will be less surprised by all the unforeseen circumstances of the change process

The costs of change in Prof. Beer's equation include shifts in power, rendering certain people and skills obsolete, changing networks of relationships, undermining people's sense of identity and in many cases reorganising an entrenched rewards system. Think of how much angst is involved in switching people's parking spaces. Then multiply that a thousand-fold when you up-end an entire division or product line. Sometimes, a company's very existence may be at stake, in such a visible way that opposition melts away. If the lights are off and the office doors padlocked by the bailiffs, even the doughtiest opponent of change might realise his mistake. But no manager wants to hit rock-bottom before changing.

It is their job to see challenges off in the distance and change course ahead of time. Everyone has to be convinced that it is worth it. Not all will be convinced immediately, and this will take months and years of effort. They will have to be led gently to a new sense of who they are and what they do. No change occurs with just one speech or memo, however elegantly worded.

Leading change can be a lonely business. Finding colleagues who agree with and understand your efforts and meeting regularly with them will be vital to maintaining morale.

Overcoming resistance

Niccolò Machiavelli wrote in *The Prince* that there is 'nothing more difficult to carry out, nor more doubtful of success, nor more dangerous to handle, than to initiate a new order of things'. Change requires reordering a status quo, which, however unpleasant it may be, will have its defenders. The promising unknown struggles in a fight with the dreary known.

Yet organisations today can expect to undergo major changes at least once every three or four years. It is simply the way the world is. Managers at every level in an organisation need to prepare for such change, to anticipate it in their own actions, and respond to it when it is imposed on them.

Opposition to change tends to take one of four forms:

1 Parochial self-interest, in which one set of employees refuse to accept change for the good of the whole company.
2 Misunderstanding and a lack of trust, engendered when managers fail to think through the consequences of their actions.

3 Difference of opinion, when people do not agree with your diagnosis of the situation and your prescribed course of treatment.

4 Low tolerance for change, when people fear they cannot acquire the new skills for the changed environment, or are simply too lazy or stubborn to go through with it.[4]

Take a very simple situation. More and more of your workers are asking if they can work from home. It would give them greater flexibility in balancing their work and family lives and advances in technology make it easy. It would also lower your costs as you could rent less office space. So one morning you come in to work and decide to announce a new flexible working schedule. Within minutes you are under siege. Everyone knows what 'flexible working' means. It means cutting back on hours, moving people out of full-time jobs with benefits and shunting them closer to the freelance economy. 'No', you insist. But your promises get no traction, especially if you have not been at the company long enough to build up a hefty store of trust.

> a classic mistake is to ignore the psychological consequences of even the most trivial-seeming change

Another classic mistake is to ignore the psychological consequences of even the most trivial-seeming change. You may think that removing desserts from the cafeteria menu and adding fruit would be welcomed by all as a move to healthier eating and lower costs. But you will inevitably face an uproar from people accusing you of meddling in their personal lives.

Cheap perks, such as taxis home for employees who stay late, may seem ripe for cutting, but their psychological value may far outweigh their monetary cost. Cut them and the message won't just be that you are a frugal manager, but that you don't value

---

[4] 'Choosing Strategies for Change', John Kotter and Leonard Schlesinger, *Harvard Business Review*, March–April 1979

your employees. If you pay a small bonus every year to your staff and suddenly don't one year, people will feel terribly betrayed and angry, disproportionately to the size of the bonus.

It is always better, then, to overestimate resistance to even the smallest change. The best way of managing resistance is to be in a process of constant improvement. Rather than being forced to change everything when your business is in trouble, you should be always educating, communicating, learning, listening and tinkering with your organisation.

You should not have to wait for a downturn to fire low-performing employees. You should be clearing house every few weeks, pruning and tending to the health of your organisation as you go. When you ask for your employees' opinion, they should not be startled. They should expect to be heard from and to be kept informed of the pressures and conditions which are influencing your actions.

In tough situations, a manager can resort to manipulating others, perhaps by giving a potentially difficult employee a key role in the change process, or ultimately even coercing them. This can be useful when there is no time for the lengthier means of persuasion, but it creates the risk that people will feel steamrollered and mistreated.

Choosing how you wish to introduce change will of course depend on the situation. If change is urgent, you may need to act quickly, alone or with the help of a small group, overcoming rather than seeking to limit resistance. If change is less urgent or is part of an ongoing process, you are best served bringing as many people along as you can and keeping the organisation whole and happy as you lead it in a new direction.

But the key requirement for a manager in either case is to have a complete grasp of the reasons for change and the stakes, the array of possible consequences and sources of resistance, and a clear strategy for dealing with that resistance in such a way that it does not derail your progress to a new state of organisational being.

Avoiding common mistakes

The second greatest mistake a manager can make when trying to change anything is to underestimate the time it will take. Think of organisational change like a home improvement. Estimate the time and cost and double them.

The greatest mistake is to deny there is a need for change in the first place.[5]

In 1926, Henry Ford was the most famous businessman in the world, a self-made billionaire who had made the car affordable to millions of Americans. He had liberated his countrymen from the horse and carriage and closed the vast distances which separated them. He had achieved all of this with a single car, the Model T. It was rugged, dependable and above all cheap. Ford achieved all this by refining his production line, continuously driving down the cost of production. He was a mechanic by training, who could assemble a Model T by himself, and he took great pride in creating his car for the masses.

But by the 1920s, American tastes had begun to change. As people became richer, they were seeking out different models of car and different colours. Cars which went beyond the Model T's utilitarian purpose and were more expressive of their personalities and needs. Families wanted family cars, and young bachelors sporty two-seaters. Meanwhile Ford was stuck. The Model T was so well built, that once someone bought one, they rarely came back for a second. The market in second-hand Model Ts thrived as the market for new ones stalled.

> Ford was committed to competing on price and reliability at a time when customers sought flair and differentiation

---

[5] The stories which follow come from *Denial: Why Business Leaders Fail to Look Facts in the Face – And What to Do About It*, Richard Tedlow, Portfolio, 2010

Furthermore, Ford was committed to competing on price and reliability at a time when customers sought flair and differentiation.

Alfred Sloan, the chief executive of General Motors, noticed this and swung into action. He introduced annual model changes to encourage car owners to upgrade their cars, even when they did not need to for purely functional purposes. GM wanted buyers to think of cars as they would clothes, an expression of your taste and status.

But when Ford's executive went and explained all of this to Henry Ford, and showed him the declining sales figures, Ford threw them out, saying their figures were nonsense. It fell to Ernest Kenzler, a senior manager at Ford, and the brother-in-law of Ford's only child, Edsel, to speak truth to power. He wrote a seven-page memo to Ford and delivered it in early 1926.

Kenzler began the memo by saying how difficult it was to write, and how much he admired Ford for his achievements. But then, he went on, 'we are losing our position because the world has learned from you and with its combined efforts, each learning from the other, it has now developed a product that is alarmingly absorbing the public's purchasing power . . . With every additional car that our competitors sell they get stronger and we get weaker . . . Inwardly we are alarmed to see our advantages ebbing away, knowing that the counter-measures to prevent it are not immediately at hand.' Ford's response? He fired his insubordinate manager and kept on making and selling the Model T. General Motors soon overtook Ford's lead in US market share and has not relinquished its position since.

Compare Ford's blunt refusal to face facts with what happened at Intel in 1985. Intel had been run since its founding in 1968 by three men, Robert Noyce, Gordon Moore and Andy Grove, who together conformed to Peter Drucker's vision of the ideal chief executive, part outsider, part thinker, part man of action. Noyce and Moore were utterly self-confident intellects and entrepreneurs.

Grove, however, had been born in Budapest in 1936, to Jewish parents. The first eight years of his life were dominated by fears of the Nazis, who between 1944 and the end of the Second World War killed over two-thirds of Hungary's Jews. The decade after the war was shaped by the tyranny and lies of Soviet influence. In 1956, at the age of 20, Grove, at the urging of his grandmother, who had survived Auschwitz, fled, leaving his family behind him. Unlike Noyce and Moore, he did not believe that hard work and intellect necessarily led to just outcomes. He believed in the title of one of his best-known works, that in both life and the technology industry 'only the paranoid survive'.

As a manager, Grove spent much of his time talking with middle managers and the sales force, the people who actually dealt with customers, because it was only here, he felt, that you could take the real pulse of the company. And problems, he believed, tended to start at the edges. Or as he put it, 'snow melts first at the periphery'.

By the mid-1980s, Intel was an undisputed technology giant. Its sales were over $1.5 billion a year, and its profits passing $200 million. Every PC being made needed a microprocessor, and Intel dominated the business. Unfortunately, Intel still saw itself as a manufacturer of memory chips rather than microprocessors. Memory had been what launched Intel, and memory was where it saw its future. By the mid-1980s, however, the Japanese were at their heels, making more memory for less and threatening Intel's traditional business. Even though Intel had a now-thriving business in microprocessors, it regarded it as secondary, and was over-investing in manufacturing memory when prices started to plummet.

Intel, Grove said, was wedded to two strongly held dogmas which were holding it back. The first was that memory remained its core product, and that everything followed by researching and investing in memory. The second dogma was that its customers demanded a full product line. The marketing department insisted that Intel could not pick and choose which products to make. Its customers insisted they make all of them.

Grove and Moore were grappling with this problem in mid-1985, feeling despondent. Grove then asked the question any manager faced with introducing change should ask: 'If we got kicked out and the board brought in a new CEO, what do you think he would do?' Without a moment's hesitation, Moore replied: 'He would get us out of memories.' To which Grove said, 'Why shouldn't you and I walk out the door, come back and do it ourselves?'

By changing their point of view, Grove had cut through the emotion which dogged the issue, answering his own question. He had become dispassionate and it allowed him to make a case based on the facts rather than feeling. By turning himself into an impartial judge of Intel's situation, he had avoided Henry Ford's fate.

It did not mean change followed effortlessly. It had to be worked through. Executives had to be persuaded. There were moments when even Grove found his resolve challenged, when he allowed research to continue into products he had decided the company could no longer afford to sell. Employees had to be fired, factories closed and customers disappointed. But to his amazement, Grove found that those middle managers and salespeople he spent so much time with, were accepting of change. They knew that it was coming.

Whereas the senior executives were focused on grand strategic issues, these people deep in the organisation had been making month-to-month decisions on manufacturing and sales which had led them to the conclusion that microprocessors were the way to go. 'These people didn't have the authority to get us out of memories but they had the authority to fine-tune the production allocation process by lots of little steps. Over the course of many months, their actions made it easier to eventually pull the plug on our memory participation.'

If managers are empowered to meet certain targets and to adjust in mid-flight, then change needn't be the great trauma it might seem.

Turning conflict into creativity

Grove's observation that his managers and salespeople were changing Intel in subtle but significant ways long before he did emphasises the need for managers to educate their employees and create in them a sense of permanent discomfort. It makes it much easier to lead change when your employees are most of the way to accepting the need for it already.

To achieve this kind of highly adaptive organisation, however, requires managers to help others orient towards the future as well as the present. It should not be just the manager reading up on new technologies and expanding and renewing his network. Every employee should be doing the same.

It is said of great athletes that they slow the game down. What to most of us seem like balls zinging from foot to foot or racquet to racquet, to the champion happens in slow motion. They don't just react, they act deliberately, fusing instinct, intellect and well-drilled talent. They see patterns where the rest of us see a blur of motion. They are thinking several moves ahead, while the amateur is focused on not messing up right now. Leadership scholars call this attitude 'getting on the balcony'.[6] It means getting up and away from your day-to-day problems and getting the right perspective on your challenges. It was what Andy Grove and Gordon Moore did at Intel.

But in a really well-functioning organisation, everyone is capable of getting on the balcony, not just the leaders. A flight attendant at an airline should be encouraged to view her daily experiences in the context of the entire airline's business. If customers are complaining about the poor quality of the coffee, it may not just be the coffee that is the problem – more likely it is a general unhappiness with the airline's approach to customer service. Managers can encourage this kind of thinking, but must also be ready to

---

[6] 'The Work of Leadership', Ronald Heifetz and Donald Laurie, *Harvard Business Review*, January 1997

listen to it when it is expressed. They must figure out whether each problem can be solved with a targeted, technical solution, or if it needs the company to adapt its entire value system.

One of the worst poisons in a company trying to change is a sense of helplessness among employees. By paying attention to others and inviting them to share in the resolution of a problem, a manager can go a long way to raising the collective intelligence of his organisation, and taking the inevitable conflicts which will arise and using them to fuel creative solutions.

Peter Guber, the Hollywood producer of such hits as *The Color Purple*, *Batman* and *Rain Man*, tells a story of when he was a young executive given the enormous task of running Columbia Pictures. He was working on a project which required him to pay a visit to Jack Warner, the founder and retired CEO of Warner Brothers. During their meeting, Warner asked him how things were going at Columbia. Guber told him he felt overwhelmed by people coming to him with their problems. Warner replied with a curious but memorable analogy.

> *It's a zoo. You're the zookeeper, and every single person that comes in the office comes with a monkey. That monkey is their problem. They're trying to leave it with you. Your job is to discover where the monkey is. They'll hide it, or dress it up, but remember you're the zookeeper. You've got to keep the place clean. So make sure when you walk them to the door, they've got their monkey by the hand. Don't let them leave without it. Don't let them come back until it's trained and they have solutions to their problem. Otherwise at the end of the day, you'll have an office full of screaming, jumping animals and monkey shit all over the floor.*[7]

People will try to dump their problems on you, the manager. Your job is to dump them right back, while giving people the tools, knowledge and encouragement to go and fix them themselves.

---

[7] *Tell to Win: Connect, Persuade and Triumph with the Hidden Power of Story*, Peter Guber, Crown Business Books, 2011, p. 149

Those who cannot work without constant hand-holding and supervision must eventually be replaced. Only by delegating can you breed an adaptable organisation, capable of self-regulation and frequent change with minimal drama. Trying to solve every problem yourself is both selfish and damaging, as inevitably you will be overwhelmed and will underperform.

Developing a vision

Corporate visions can easily become the targets of ridicule. Pompous CEOs love to talk about the five-year vision, and spout pieties about their company which have no basis in reality. Enron was big on vision right up to its implosion. Just two months before the company's well-hidden problems were starting to emerge, Enron's chairman, Kenneth Lay, wrote a letter to his employees urging them to buy the company's stock: 'Our performance has never been stronger; our business model has never been more robust. . . . We have the finest organization in American business today.'

Enron had a 64-page Code of Ethics document and a shorter 'Vision and Values' statement, the 'V&V' for short, which claimed that: 'As a partner in the communities in which we operate, Enron believes it has a responsibility to conduct itself according to certain basic principles.' Enron said it was a 'global corporate citizen' with four core values: respect, integrity, communication and excellence. 'We treat others as we would like to be treated ourselves', said the V&V. 'We do not tolerate abusive or disrespectful treatment. Ruthlessness, callousness and arrogance don't belong here.'

It is not hard to see why such boasts cause eye-rolling among many employees.

But contrast that with one of the most famous and enduring statements of corporate values, the HP Way of Hewlett-Packard, which was drafted by the company's co-founder, David Packard:

The HP Way

We have trust and respect for individuals.

We approach each situation with the belief that people want to do a good job and will do so, given the proper tools and support. We attract highly capable, diverse, innovative people and recognize their efforts and contributions to the company. HP people contribute enthusiastically and share in the success that they make possible.

We focus on a high level of achievement and contribution.

Our customers expect HP products and services to be of the highest quality and to provide lasting value. To achieve this, all HP people, especially managers, must be leaders who generate enthusiasm and respond with extra effort to meet customer needs. Techniques and management practices which are effective today may be outdated in the future. For us to remain at the forefront in all our activities, people should always be looking for new and better ways to do their work.

We conduct our business with uncompromising integrity.

We expect HP people to be open and honest in their dealings to earn the trust and loyalty of others. People at every level are expected to adhere to the highest standards of business ethics and must understand that anything less is unacceptable. As a practical matter, ethical conduct cannot be assured by written HP policies and codes; it must be an integral part of the organization, a deeply ingrained tradition that is passed from one generation of employees to another.

We achieve our common objectives through teamwork.

We recognize that it is only through effective cooperation within and among organizations that we can achieve our goals. Our commitment is to work as a worldwide team to fulfill the expectations of our customers, shareholders and others who depend upon us. The benefits and obligations of doing business are shared among all HP people.

We encourage flexibility and innovation.

We create an inclusive work environment which supports the diversity of our people and stimulates innovation. We strive for overall objectives which are clearly stated and agreed upon, and allow people flexibility in working toward goals in ways that they help determine are best for the organization. HP people should personally accept responsibility and be encouraged to upgrade their skills and capabilities through ongoing training and development. This is especially important in a technical business where the rate of progress is rapid and where people are expected to adapt to change.

Compare the specificity and modesty of the HP Way with the vacuity and hubris of Enron's V&V statement and consider which one is closer to your own organisation's. Hewlett-Packard's culture was forged by the founders' experiences and personalities forged in the Second World War and the years which followed. After the war, David Packard and William Hewlett had to lay off staff, an experience they found so traumatic that they vowed never to do so again. They didn't for the next forty years. HP's winning thesis was to compete only in new technology markets where it could be market-dominant and stay ahead of the competition through continual innovation and better quality, and thus charge a higher price. For decades, all of HP's employees could carry a model in their own mind of how their company worked. It was consistent and straightforward and worthy of their trust.

Jim Collins describes a well-conceived vision as one that has two main pieces, 'core ideology and envisioned future'.[8] A core ideology is something like the HP Way, which describes what you are in business for. In Hewlett-Packard's case it was to create great products for the good of humanity, and a healthy, decent, high-achieving company. Ideologies like these can survive any number of external changes to markets, customers and product

---

[8] 'Building your Company's Vision', James Collins and Jerry Porras, *Harvard Business Review*, October 1996

needs. The Walt Disney Company, for all that has changed in the media business since its founding, retains its faith in imagination and wholesomeness and an abhorrence for cynicism. Core values might from time to time become an impediment to business success, but they survive because they are what give a company's employees purpose. They inspire people to come to work not to meet this quarter's target but to do something meaningful with their lives through the means of the organisation they work for.

> ideologies like these can survive any number of external changes to markets

A bank which says its purpose is to charge people fees for looking after and lending them money is merely describing its primary activities. What it is really doing, provided it is honest, is helping society grow by giving people the financial stability essential to building wealth. Earnings per share should be the last thing on people's minds when they explain to you their company's purpose.

If you cannot figure this out, Collins suggests the following: imagine someone came and offered you a very good price for your company, and everyone agreed it should be sold. But the day after the purchase, the buyer shut your company down, eradicating its brands and products. What would be lost to the world? Would you even care? If you don't, you have no core values or ideology. If you do, the reason why you do is the core of what you do each day.

Defining core values and ideologies may seem more like the work of CEOs and boards than of mid-level managers. But if you are to do your work with any enthusiasm or encourage others, you need to know why you are doing it, even if your bosses articulate it poorly.

The second key part of a vision, according to Collins, is an 'envisioned future' and preferably an extremely ambitious one. It is not enough to say you want to build an OK company and make some money. You need to talk more like Steve Jobs, of 'putting a dent in the universe' with your products, or 'organizing the world's information' like Google. Aspire to greatness, and even if you fall short, you will be far ahead of those who simply aim to be average. A compelling goal, like President Kennedy's declaration in 1962 that by the end of the decade the United States would put a man on the moon, needs no further explanation. This was, by Collins's definition, such a BHAG, a big, hairy, audacious goal, that everyone got it immediately and rallied round. The last thing a BHAG needs to be is a sure thing. In fact it should seem out of reach, excitingly so, so your employees leap out of bed each morning feeling they are part of something big, however daunting the odds.

In June 1940, as Germany's armed forces were sweeping ominously through Europe, Winston Churchill elevated the nature and likely duration of the struggle to epic proportions. The fighter pilots who flew each day to guard Britain's skies made the Knights of the Round Table look prosaic. As for the prospect of defeat, it was inconceivable:

> *Even though large tracts of Europe and many old and famous States have fallen or may fall into the grip of the Gestapo and all the odious apparatus of Nazi rule, we shall not flag or fail. We shall go on to the end, we shall fight in France, we shall fight on the seas and oceans, we shall fight with growing confidence and growing strength in the air, we shall defend our Island, whatever the cost may be, we shall fight on the beaches, we shall fight on the landing grounds, we shall fight in the fields and in the streets, we shall fight in the hills; we shall never surrender, and even if, which I do not for a moment believe, this Island or a large part of it were subjugated and starving, then our Empire beyond the seas, armed and guarded by the British Fleet, would carry on the struggle, until, in God's good time, the New World, with all its power and might, steps forth to the rescue and the liberation of the old.*

As BHAGs go, Churchill's speech in Parliament on 4 June 1940 was as good as it gets, vivid, inspiring and memorable. It allowed him to lead the country through the wrenching change of wartime.

A powerful vision helps people understand the need for change and the means by which it will be achieved. It carries them over the inevitable obstacles. A CEO may articulate that vision, but it is up to every manager to repeat it and make it realisable through practical steps taken every hour, day and week.

> a powerful vision helps people to understand the need for change and carries them over the inevitable

Harnessing the power of stories

When Bill Clinton was running for the US Presidency in 1992, his campaign was very nearly torpedoed by rumours that he dodged the Vietnam draft and had cheated repeatedly on his wife. When he lost the New Hampshire Democratic Primary, many wrote him off for dead. There was no way this man could be chosen as his party's nominee, let alone President. Clinton, however, has long believed that politics is the art of 'giving people better stories'. Stories which help explain their present condition and paths to a better future, and stories about those who wish to lead them. Stories are also currency which can easily be passed along and traded.

To salvage his campaign, Clinton had to raise more money from discouraged supporters and press on. He needed a great story. When a Hollywood supporter asked Clinton if he thought he could still win, Clinton said 'this is High Noon'. The 1952 movie *High Noon* tells the story of a small-town sheriff who decided to stay and fight the criminal gang arriving on the noon train. Everyone in the town abandons him but a young boy. For a Hollywood executive, this was exactly the right story, and immediately he picked up the phone and began passing the story along to other potential contributors. Bill Clinton was the sheriff, and each of you can choose to be either the cowardly townsfolk or the fearless young boy. By the end of the afternoon, the executive had raised the $90,000 asked of him. He called the Clinton campaign and said: 'It's High Noon and you've got your money. Now take on the bad guys.'[9]

As a manager trying to create urgency and implement change, you should try to frame your challenge as a story which people can easily pass along to others. No one passes on a PowerPoint presentation or a blur of numbers at the water cooler. But they do pass along stories which amuse, enlighten or scare others into action. Everyone wants interesting stories to tell their friends and colleagues.

If you can turn your problems and solutions into stories like Clinton's High Noon, you will have raised the chances of turning your ambitions into results.

Achieving cultural continuity[10]

Change is not always about turning over the tables and embracing the new. In some cases it involves moving forward by going back to the past.

In late 2010, a group of American investors decided to buy Liverpool Football Club from another set of American owners who had grievously mismanaged it, loading it up with debt and failing to win the trophies expected by the club's fans. Over the course of its history, Liverpool had experienced the highest highs – European Cups and a record number of domestic championships – and the lowest lows – hooliganism and the Heysel and Hillsborough stadium disasters in which scores of fans lost their lives. One of the club's great managers, Bill Shankly, summed up life at Liverpool when he said 'some people think football is a matter of life and death. I assure you, it's much more serious than that.'

---

[9] *Tell to Win: Connect, Persuade and Triumph with the Hidden Power of Story*, Peter Guber, Crown Business Books, 2011, p. 121

[10] Parts of this section are taken from Delves Broughton, P., 'The winning tactic of cultural continuity', *The Financial Times*, 11 October 2010. © The Financial Times 2010. All rights reserved. For the full article, see the appendix at the back of the book.

The new owners of Liverpool came to the club with a formidable bench of talent. The leader of the group was John Henry, a wealthy trader who had bought the Boston Red Sox baseball club and turned it into a winner after more than eighty years of futility. The other investors were Jeffrey Vinik, the former manager of Fidelity's gargantuan Magellan Fund turned successful hedge fund manager; Michael Gordon, Mr Vinik's former partner; David Ginsberg, one of Mr Henry's former fund managers, and Tom Werner, the producer of television mega-series such as *The Cosby Show* and *Roseanne*. Mr Henry also had at his disposal Michael Porter, his strategy adviser at the Boston Red Sox and the world's most influential business academic.

Applying his widely taught Five Forces analysis to measure the attractiveness of English football, Prof. Porter would have found that its competitive rivalry is intense, measured week after week by results on the pitch as well as on income statements. The threat of new entrants is low, as the same handful of clubs tend to dominate European football year after year. The threat of substitutes is equally small, as football fans are not easily swayed to other sports. The bargaining power of customers is low as fans rarely switch allegiance, and sponsors and broadcasters are desperate to tap into the sport's popularity.

Unfortunately, the bargaining power of suppliers, the players, is where football's economic attractiveness breaks down. Wage inflation made it hard for even the most successful clubs to turn a large profit. As Deloitte said in its 2010 Review on Football Finance: 'We [are] seeing a continuing shift from a sustainable "not for profit" model towards one with potentially calamitous, consistent and significant lossmaking characteristics.'

Three business models had surfaced in English football in the years leading up to Liverpool's acquisition by Henry and his group. The open chequebook model at Chelsea and Manchester City, where a multi-billionaire owner decides to spend whatever it takes to buy success. The leveraged buy-out model, at Manchester United and Liverpool, where foreign owners hobble their clubs with debt and find themselves loathed by fans. And finally the Arsenal model, where a steady management focuses on cash flow from player transfers and property, as well as the usual tickets, merchandise and broadcast rights, and remains competitive without straining to win at all costs.

Mr Henry bought Liverpool for a good price. The club still had devoted fans and extraordinary players. But he did not have the billions of Chelsea and, after Liverpool's near bankruptcy, was not going to find borrowing easy. As another American buying a British team, his leash with the fans would be short.

His first move, then, was to show that despite being an outsider, he understood the importance of the club's history, and he reached back to appoint a manager with roots in its once-fabled management system. From the 1960s to the 1990s, Liverpool's glory years, the heart of this system was 'the boot room'. Conjuring up images of muddy tracksuits and stewing tea, it was the room where managers, coaches and senior players would gather and talk. After matches, opposing managers were invited as well. The boot room was where winning habits were set and future managers trained. It created cultural continuity, and just as at General Electric, Liverpool's boot room was about promoting from within.

But in the late 1990s, after some mediocre years, Liverpool abandoned the boot room. It hired outside managers who failed to restore the club's edge. John Henry reversed this process, by appointing Kenny Dalglish as his manager, a revered former player and manager who understood all that the Liverpool boot room stood for. The fans loved it as it restored a sense of stability to the club. Change in football would be inevitable. But in order to move forward, it served Henry well to step back, to examine the culture of his acquisition and to build on it. Whatever changes he makes in the future can now rest on this firm foundation of cultural continuity.

Managing disruptive change

In his book *The Structure of Scientific Revolutions*, the late historian Thomas Kuhn argued that great advances in science did not emerge from a smooth process of endless and accretive experimentation. Rather they tended to come in short, sharp, uncomfortable bursts, which turned all existing thinking on its head.

For centuries scientists believed that Aristotle had been right in his belief that the sun revolved around the earth. When Galileo challenged this idea, he was hauled before a papal court in Rome, ordered to 'abject, curse and detest' his radical opinions and sentenced to house arrest for the rest of his life, so he could not spread his heretical ideas.

Kuhn wrote that science tends to work in paradigms, rigid models of belief. Experiments are conducted and scientists form a culture which supports the paradigm. Anomalies may crop up, but they are treated as just that, exceptions to the rule which don't change the underlying model. Then every so often, someone comes along and offers up a new paradigm, a Galileo, Newton or Einstein. They are mocked and rebuffed at first, but eventually accepted as their theory makes sense of the anomalies which have been piling up over the years. This process of acceptance can take years, as scientists make the slow move from the old to the new.

> every so often, someone comes along and offers up a new paradigm

In business, much the same happens. Most businesses are deeply conservative, following the same practices and trusting the same ideas as everyone else. Until someone comes along and does it completely differently, a Sam Walton with Wal-Mart, perhaps, or a Steve Jobs with Apple or a Michael O'Leary with Ryanair.

Suddenly, all the prices and inconveniences we used to put up with seem absurd.

During the 1960s, a great leap forward was made for patients suffering from blocked arteries, the cause of heart disease. Cardiac surgeons found a way to reroute blood around the blockages, but it required sawing open a patient's rib cage to get to the heart. It was a hugely complicated procedure, which required a long recovery time, but if successful it could add years to a patient's life. Then in 1974, a young German doctor, Andreas Gruentzig, discovered a different way of fixing an arterial blockage. He inserted a small balloon into the blocked vein, inflated it so it pressed out the plaque hindering the flow of blood, then removed it. It was much simpler and less traumatic for the patient.

Cardiac surgeons initially dismissed the process, called 'balloon angioplasty', because it was far less remunerative for them and could not be used on their core set of patients, people with heart disease so serious they required surgery. A different group of doctors – cardiologists – however, were much more enthusiastic. The new procedure was one they could administer, which meant they could do much more to treat their patients, and be reimbursed at a higher rate.

For the next two decades, both procedures, surgery and angioplasty, grew in popularity. But as angioplasty became increasingly sophisticated it began to be used in ever more serious cases of heart disease. By 1995, the number of balloon angioplasties passed the number of bypass surgeries. Cardiologists had staged a successful disruption of their industry, by finding a large group of new customers willing to try a simpler new technology.

This was a classic disruption. But we have seen it in all kinds of industries. Disruption occurs when an established player, or business model, has begun to offer too much to its existing customers, thereby creating an opportunity for a new entrant with a simpler, cheaper product. The established player will see and understand the threat, but they are so wedded to their existing business model and level of profitability that they cannot adjust to seize the new opportunity themselves. Over time, the new entrant gains knowledge and customers, develops its product and eventually overtakes the once-entrenched market leader.[11]

Take the print newspaper industry. When digital publishing took off in the 1990s, print publishers invested millions creating and marketing their websites. They understood the impact of the Internet and feared their customers would move online, where production costs were cheaper, leaving them stuck with expensive printing presses and delivery networks. The only problem was that they tried simply to move the print model of content supported by advertising online. They failed to see that the nature of both content and advertising changed dramatically in the shift from print to the Internet. Traditional newspaper advertisers, like car companies and department stores, were unwilling to pay the same rates they paid for print ads for online versions. And readers found they no longer needed a single source of news any more once they could piece together their own 'Daily Me' from multiple sources online.

Meanwhile, companies which had been born online, without the legacy of print, went about the business very differently. Companies like CNET mixed original and repackaged content, they invited sharing and user interaction. They also went after very different kinds of advertisers, those who wanted to target very specific groups of consumers, rather than the mass audience targeted by a print ad. It was the difference between an advertisement on Google delivered to a reader based on their unique interests, and a department store ad in a newspaper trumpeting a weekend mattress sale.

Newspapers sought to innovate to protect their lucrative existing businesses. The new entrants were seeking entirely new sets of customers, both readers and advertisers, with a different product,

---

[11] 'Foundations for Growth: How to Identify and Build Disruptive New Businesses', C.M. Christensen, M.W. Johnson and D.K. Rigby, *MIT Sloan Management Review 43*, Spring 2002, pp. 22–31

delivered at lower cost and requiring very different levels of revenue to be profitable.

We see it happening every day in one industry or another. Google has started offering free productivity software for writing documents and creating spreadsheets, which Microsoft has traditionally charged for. Google's product is evidently less sophisticated, but it may be all many people need. Not everyone needs all the bells and whistles which come with Microsoft's Word and Excel. Google makes its money on advertising to those who use its free software, whereas Microsoft still depends on selling the software. These processes take time, but it becomes harder and harder to envisage a time when the majority of computer users are not using free productivity software.

Managers will always struggle to manage disruption. It is, self-evidently, disruptive, forcing unwanted change and overturning what may be very comfortable and lucrative business models. It is also slow-acting, which can create complacency. You might think you have it under control, until years later, without you every quite realising, you find the market has changed and you have been usurped. It also requires a very different mindset, an entrepreneurial knack for marshalling and channelling new resources, for experimenting and iterating at low cost until you have found the right product for the right customer. Anyone who has grown up in a large company where resources are abundant, and ideas evolved over rounds of endless meetings, might mistake disruptive innovation for just another kind of new product launch. It isn't.

Managers, then, need to understand the following about disruptive innovation:

● It works when it follows the needs of the new customer. Established products come with all kinds of legacy costs and features that no one values. New products can be driven entirely by what the new market wants and is willing to pay for. New customers are not the ones disrupted by new products. They will embrace them if they are genuinely useful and different.

- New customers for disruptive products are not your old customers, but those who are not consuming the existing products. Before balloon angioplasty, people with mild heart disease were not getting more limited forms of surgery, they were getting no surgery at all.

- Disruptive innovations should start small and be allowed to grow slowly. Patience will give managers time to understand what customers want and how to deliver it most efficiently. This will require experimentation. It won't work by throwing buckets of money at the first idea and hoping you can shove it through the existing channels of distribution.

- And finally, disruption always ends up expanding the market. It may lead to incumbents losing their place, and lower prices for old products, but over time it brings in more consumers, expands the range of products and makes for a bigger market for everyone. Managers who understand this will have less to fear in the change disruption brings.

Top 10 tips for managing change

1 Regard change as a constant process rather than a sudden bolt from the blue.

2 Create a sense of crisis or urgency. Without it no change can happen.

3 Understand the cultural changes that must be made as well as the business ones. Changing a dress code can have as dramatic an effect as changing the product line.

4 Expect resistance and develop a strategy to overcome it, ideally by learning yourself and educating your staff to understand the reasons for change before it happens.

5 In the face of a difficult change, ask yourself the Intel question: if a new manager were to come in and face this situation what would he do? This allows you to be dispassionate.

▶

6   Learn to recognise denial in yourself and those around you. Are you ignoring facts or ideas because they are wrong, or because they don't fit your comfortable vision of the world?

7   Be specific about the changes you need. Be more like the old HP Way than Enron.

8   Use inspiring visions and stories to bring people along with you.

9   Make sure you recognise what in the past is valuable before you decide to throw it out.

10 Look out for disruptive challengers and collaborate with them rather than try to defend against them.

Chapter 6
Managing strategy

What topics are covered in this chapter?

- Putting corporate strategy into action
- Moving innovation centre stage
- Allowing both success and failure
- Learning from the past
- Keeping success in check

Most managers are handed a strategy and instructed to implement it. In some companies they may be invited to contribute to the strategic plan, but their ideas will then be bundled up into a scheme dreamed up in the corporate suite, by youthful 'strategic planners' who imagine a company's future with little regard for how it might come to pass.

Senior executives often enjoy strategic planning, because it lifts them out of the grind of the present and offers them a chance to dream of a rosier future. Investors like to see a strategic plan because it helps inform a stock price, which is nothing more than the market's view of the present value of estimated future earnings. Stock prices and strategy are both forms of wishful thinking about a company's future.

Despite this, strategy is not entirely meaningless. It can offer a broad set of goals, identify new opportunities and provide ideas for how they might be approached. But it can also inspire profound cynicism. I've heard executives say that the only purpose of a strategy document is to have something to pull out of a drawer when the board asks about your strategy. Others consider it an even greater waste of time, shifting organisational focus from the here and now to plans which could only ever be fulfilled in the febrile fantasies of management consultants.

Any investment of time or resources with no obvious payback is all too often excused as 'strategic', to the despair of managers putting out daily fires under extreme constraints.

Nonetheless, it is worth every manager understanding something of strategy, if only because it helps explain why each business is as it is. Strategy as a form of corporate daydreaming may be of dubious value, but strategy as a means of understanding the forces which shape your company today can be extremely useful.

Understanding strategy

But before one does anything else, it is worth asking: what is strategy? The term was first applied to business as recently as 1962 by the historian Alfred Chandler in his book *Strategy and Structure: Chapters in the History of the American Industrial Enterprise.*

Looking back at the history of some of America's greatest corporations, Chandler defined strategy as the determination of long-term goals and the adoption of certain actions to achieve them. The structure of organisations, the lines of command and information flow, then followed these strategic goals.

The 1960s was a very confusing decade for American business. The economic and social certainties of the 1950s gave way to faster change and an overturning of many orthodoxies. This process only quickened in subsequent decades. Businesses which had ridden the emergence of America's consumer mass market for most of the 20th century now found their beliefs and business models being undermined by changing tastes, foreign competition and new, fast-growing technology start-ups. All of this drove executives into the waiting arms of management consultants, a still-new profession, whose data-driven models and strategic plans, echoing those of great wartime generals, had the air of intellectual certainty. Business strategy in its earliest days was an action plan for growth based on a detailed understanding of a company's markets, rivals, capabilities and customers. Vast planning departments were created with the job of mapping a company's position. Those in operations often regarded these planners and their maps with contempt.

The response came a few years later with the emergence of an 'execution' school of strategists. They argued that by focusing on developing market share and short-term financial growth, companies missed the real point of strategy, which was to develop long-term sustainable advantage. Their thinking was framed by observing Swiss, French and German machine-tool manufacturers, whose use of computers and other technologies put them far ahead of their American rivals.

Even with many of the same social and labour conditions as American companies, these European firms were winning through superb operations. Strategy under this view became an intense focus on process improvement, on analysing every piece of a company's actions and seeking to make them better, getting rid of waste and enhancing the lives of employees by fully engaging them in their work.

But even that came to seem a very reduced view of strategy. Strategy has now evolved into a collective term for the complex set of interactions which create the gap between a company's costs and its customers' willingness to pay. A successful strategy allows a company to create a wider gap than its competitors for the same set of customers. Understanding a company's position and operational excellence are just two parts of what makes a great strategy. The magic happens when managers put all the pieces together.

> a successful strategy allows a company to create a wider gap than its competition for the same set of customers

Consider Tesco. Its strategy is not just to provide great food at great prices. It isn't even just to make them loyal through its Clubcard scheme. Its strategy is the whole set of activities which cumulatively create a very specific shopping experience, made up of low prices, fresh, varied and available products, enabled by great marketing, logistics and in-store and executive management.

The Clubcard scheme, for example, not only rewards customers with savings, but also allows Tesco to know what products to stock where, which makes its sourcing, shipping and storage all the more effective. It makes its entire supply chain more efficient, and enables Tesco to pass on those savings to customers. A rival which knew less about the tastes and habits of its customers would end up with more spoiled food and thus higher costs. The Clubcard generates the information which leads to better selection and lower prices, which in turn intensifies the loyalty of shoppers.

Similarly, Ryanair's rock-bottom air fares result from the company's absolute focus on stripping costs from their airline operations. It learned many of its practices from America's Southwest Airlines, using the same planes on every route to make maintenance simpler, letting employees dress comfortably, allowing passengers to find their own seat rather than receiving a seat assignment, getting rid of anything which might slow down plane turnaround times, such as seat-back pockets. The company's offices are spartan, its policies brutally clear – no refunds means no refunds. That is what you get for a £5 plane ticket. When established rivals try to enter the low-cost airline market, they fail consistently, because unlike Ryanair they are not designed top to bottom to strip out costs and pass those savings on to flyers. If you try to shove a low-cost airline into an otherwise high-cost structure, it won't work.

The forces which determine the best web of activities collectively called 'strategy' were famously enumerated by the Harvard professor, Michael Porter. He wrote that there are five basic forces which determine the intensity of competition in any industry, and that the relative strengths or weaknesses of those forces explains how a company does or should behave.

These Five Forces are:

- The threat of new entrants
- The bargaining power of customers

- The threat of substitute products or services
- The bargaining power of suppliers
- The jockeying for position among current competitors in an industry.

In certain industries, such as steel production or tyre manufacturing, the forces are intense because the returns on investment are small. In others, such as oil services or soft drinks, the effect of the forces is milder, as there is greater opportunity to make decent returns. The weaker the forces, the greater your chances at achieving long-term, sustainable profits.

This cuts straight to one of Porter's key points, that each industry has certain profitability traits that are very hard to buck. Pharmaceutical companies, for example, have consistently made much higher profits than airlines, a terrible industry, hostage to fluctuations in oil prices and passenger behaviour. Once you are in an industry, you must then make the best of managing the Five Forces which assault you, understanding them and then formulating a way to deal with them one by one. Excellent execution, according to Porter, will only take you so far. That limit is set by the nature and structure of the business you are in in the first place.

Strategy under this view becomes the process of understanding the Five Forces and finding a way to defend against them or clear out a place where you will be least buffeted by them. Ryanair in Europe and Southwest Airlines in the United States succeeded in a difficult industry by focusing on simplicity and rejecting traditional airline behaviours. They did not try to do what big, existing airlines were doing, only better. They re-imagined what passengers sought from an airline – low cost, no frills, a 'get me from A to B' service – and built their organisations around these basic principles.

As Porter put it, 'the essence of strategy is choosing to perform activities differently than rivals do'.

He used the example of IKEA, the Swedish furniture retailer. Most furniture chains offer showrooms where salespeople show customers samples of their product line and invite them to customise these samples from pictures and swatch books before placing an order for a piece of furniture which might arrive in 8 weeks. IKEA invited customers to help themselves, to wander around vast warehouses filled with room settings. Every product is on display and customers can pick up what they want, and take it home that day and assemble it themselves. IKEA offers child care and extended hours to help customers with families who spend the day working. Its services, prices and products are highly tailored to its customers. IKEA's marketing concept of offering young furniture buyers stylish products at low prices becomes strategy, Porter wrote, through the 'tailored set of activities that make it work'.

A great strategy, then, is a process of defining a position in the market, informed by understanding the Five Forces, deciding what to do and what not to do, and then making your activities fit together seamlessly and logically. This is the manager's strategic work.

A third school of strategy which emerged in the early 1990s describes it as the process of managers adapting creatively to changing circumstances. The leading advocate of this school, Henry Mintzberg, a management professor at Canada's McGill University, wrote that great managers probe into the future by letting 'a thousand strategic flowers bloom ... [using] an insightful style, to detect the patterns of success in these gardens of strategic flowers, rather than a cerebral style that favors analytical techniques to develop strategies in a hothouse'. The appeal of this view is that it defines strategy in terms of a specific managerial attitude and approach, consistent with other healthy managerial behaviours such as the bias for action over inaction and alertness to change. Its main danger is that it leads to managerial confusion and a loss of focus. A thousand flowers are a lot to watch over, especially when you have the day's business to attend to.

The fourth main school of strategy argues that the best companies succeed when they focus on their 'core competencies', the basic skills and capabilities at which they excel.[1] This could be a set of employee talents, a unique technology or a form of financial engineering. Companies which develop their strategy based on these competencies stand a good chance of winning. This makes a lot of intuitive sense. Each of us succeeds when we do what we are best at, rather than reaching into fields where we have neither skills nor experience. Companies which branch out into different lines of business in pursuit of growth may find they lack the skills to succeed. A great chef, for example, may fail when he tries to franchise his restaurant because his talents flourish behind a stove, not in the boardroom. Technology companies like Dell and Microsoft have failed when they have tried to develop their own shops, because they lack any flair for retail.

But this does not mean companies should only have one product or service. Richard Branson's Virgin Group has developed businesses in a huge range of sectors, ranging from music and travel to mobile phones, transport and financial services. Its core competence, however, is not in any one of these businesses. It is in developing and managing brands. In fact, it describes itself as a 'branded venture capital organisation' which stands for 'value for money, quality, fun and a sense of competitive challenge'. It analyses opportunities, picks its markets and asks if it can add value by applying its brand attributes and talent. Once a new venture is up and running, it can exploit the commercial value of the Virgin name, Virgin's uniquely open management style and the reputation and marketing gifts of Virgin's founder, Richard Branson. By understanding its core competence, by 2011, Virgin had created more than 300 branded companies in 30 countries, employing around 50,000 people, generating annual revenues of more than £11 billion.

---

[1] *Competing for the Future*, Gary Hamel and C.K. Prahalad, Harvard Business School Press, 1996

Until they reach the upper echelons of their company, most managers will have little to do with corporate strategy. (This should not be confused with the 'strat plan' demanded of managers, which is just a set of tactics intended to fulfil the preordained corporate strategy.) But they should understand what goes into a strategy, why it is the way it is, and how it might change. It is a rare company that develops a strategy first time out and sticks to it successfully through thick and thin.

Most strategies emerge through a process of intelligent trial and error, as senior managers develop hypotheses, experiment and move on quickly if they fail. It was only three years after Google was founded that the company came up with AdWords, the advertising model responsible for most of its revenue. Even then, few were convinced that users of search engines would appreciate having ads accompany their searches. Once it became clear that they didn't mind and that it even made search more effective, Google increased its bet on the strategy. But it wasn't a strategy that emerged fully formed from planning sessions.

> most strategies emerge through a process of intelligent trial and error

Managers searching for good strategies should be alert to certain obvious opportunities: regulatory changes; technology changes; large groups of under-served or over-served customers. Strategic opportunities are often much more obvious than they seem.

Managing open innovation

One of the great curses of corporate life is the 'not invented here' mentality. If no one at the company came up with a certain idea, then it is not worth pursuing. Narrow-minded as it is, it is all-pervasive. At a time when it was easier to protect one's markets, products and distribution channels, managers who thought like this could get away with it. Not any more. By keeping the world at arm's length, managers are putting themselves at a severe operational and strategic disadvantage. The newly conceived process known as 'open innovation' shows how.

Open innovation is the process of looking beyond your own organisation for ideas on how to improve. Or, to quote Bill Joy, co-founder of Sun Microsystems, it is a way of dealing with the fact that 'not all the smart people in the world work for you'. Surprising numbers of managers will find reasons not to look outside for ideas. They will find excuses as to why what works for others will never work for them. The situation is always different for them.

But with innovation, as with so much else in modern management, technology provides an insight into where the world is moving. We are seeing an almost barrier-less world emerging of Internet-based communication and information sharing. Armies of innovators and creators, each with their own peculiar set of motivations, contribute to Wikipedia and Linux, the open-source software platform. Companies like Apple have enjoyed great success by inviting outsiders into their own innovation process. Apple's App Store for its iPhones and iPads is filled by thousands of third-party developers who are using Apple's platform in ways the company could never have imagined, thereby increasing its value to consumers.

Another 'open innovation' approach was tried by Netflix in 2009, when it offered $1 million to anyone who could improve the quality of its film recommendations for users. The X Prize Foundation has run similar contests to stimulate advances in genomics, private space travel and alternative energy. Such contests try to draw the best minds in the world to problems they might otherwise ignore.

Procter & Gamble boasts that in the first decade of this century it went from a 'not invented here' defensiveness to a spirit of 'proudly found elsewhere', by acquiring innovative products and processes from beyond its normal corporate channels. In order to do this, P&G makes its needs and interests widely known and then invites people to come up with ideas. It then has to be ready to respond to the ideas. If a start-up comes to them with a proposition, P&G cannot spend months considering it, as the start-up could die in that time. Its managers also need to be able to help their internal organisation adapt to ideas coming from outside. It is no good letting all kinds of ideas sluice into P&G and hoping they find their way into products. Managers at every level of the organisation need to be encouraged and helped to welcome and implement these ideas, otherwise 'open innovation' becomes nothing more than a buzz term. All these internal changes, however, are worth it if P&G can put itself in a position to take advantage of innovation wherever and whenever it happens.

A cautionary tale of open innovation gone wrong was Boeing's development of its Dreamliner 787 passenger aircraft. In order to build the plane more cheaply, Boeing syndicated much of the design to outside companies. The idea was that these outsiders would make the investments in R&D and then recoup them through their subcontracts for the building of the plane. Unfortunately, the technical difficulties of integrating so many different parts got away from Boeing. When they put them all together, the 787 wouldn't fly. The complexity of the project overwhelmed the benefits of making the process open to so many companies outside Boeing.

Getting open innovation right requires a classic managerial balancing act between delegation and control. Yes, you want to remain open to as many ideas and influences as possible, but at some point, the investment has to be made, the work has to be done, and the manager has to coordinate the activities of his business so that they work seamlessly towards a common purpose.

> getting innovation right requires a ... balancing act between delegation and control

Coming at the same idea from another direction, Nike created the GreenXChange in 2010 to share some of its technological innovations with people who might be able to use them in various fields. Nike learns a great deal about materials in making its athletics gear, much of which may be useful for people in businesses unconnected to their own. Lessons from making rubber-soled shoes, for example, can be applied in developing cheap roofing materials in developing countries. By letting others use its own inventions, when it doesn't have to, Nike is enhancing its own reputation and inviting a whole network of innovators to participate in its own innovation processes, with no guaranteed return but the hunch that something good is bound to come from such intellectual and commercial friendliness.

Any time a manager releases the controls is bound to be scary. But our ordinary lives are already moving ever faster towards openness, sharing and the breakdown of once insuperable walls of privacy and control. Managers must follow.

Managing failure

No one likes to fail. And yet it has become a popular business mantra that failure is vital to success. If you never fail, you will never succeed. This is true, to an extent, but companies are rarely good at creating a culture where people feel comfortable failing. A CEO can talk about the importance of failure all he likes, but if his people worry that if they fail they will lose their job, or see their career prospects dimmed, they are unlikely to heed his words. The confusion about failure arises from a basic lack of definition. There are good and bad failures in business, avoidable and expected, stupid and intelligent, and grouping them all together is unhelpful.

Bad failures are those which result from human negligence or criminality. A failure to file paperwork on time, which leads to the loss of an important sale, is to be punished rather than celebrated. On the other hand, failures in complex hypothesis testing are essential to reaching an eventual conclusion. Innovation requires experimentation which requires failure. A company which never experiments is unlikely ever to develop a sustainable competitive advantage. It will simply plod along doing the same old thing. Good failure is that which helps you home in on an eventual success, whether by reducing options or helping you learn more about your subject.

Managers should only want to fail if by doing so they enhance their own and their organisation's eventual chances of success. Otherwise, it is best avoided.

Failure needs to be properly set up. If you are taking on a risky endeavour, be clear at the start about what you are doing. Explain to your colleagues the purpose of your action and make sure you secure the support of those above you to commit resources to a project which might in all likelihood fail. Make sure everyone shares the same expectations about the outcome. What are the odds of success? If they are low, what's the point? What do you plan to learn? What measures are you taking to minimise the risk of failure? If you draw focus to the process rather than the outcome, and you execute the process as promised, you can always call that a success, even if the outcome is a failure.

As you try to persuade others to sign up to a potential failure, make sure they feel comfortable. Each night they will be going home to families and friends and explaining what they are doing at work. Make sure they're not going home and saying, 'I've been assigned to a probable failure.' They will soon be looking for work elsewhere. You want them thinking 'I'm doing some really interesting work which no one else has done, and if it works, great, but if it doesn't I'll still be rewarded for taking on a challenge and helping my organisation get better.'

One way to ensure this is to see that everyone involved in a high-risk project has clear roles. Again, this is about the importance of process. If people have clearly defined roles and tasks which they fulfil to the best of their ability, they can feel a sense of competence and professional satisfaction even if their collective effort does not buck the odds and results in a failure. Just as in Toyota's production system, you want your employees to feel that participating in a failure or even just spotting

see that everyone involved in a high-risk project has a clear role

one, can lead eventually to a better functioning organisation.

Creating such a culture is one of the hardest tasks a manager can face. When Alan Mulally first arrived to be CEO of Ford, the car company was losing billions of dollars a year. To help him understand what was going on, Mulally asked to receive reports on the company's separate operations, 300 or so of them, marked green for progress, yellow for caution and red for problematic. For the first few weeks, all the reports came in marked green. Eventually, in frustration at his managers, he asked: 'Isn't anything NOT going well?' He soon received his first yellow report, which he welcomed with applause and soon after many more yellow and red reports followed.

Getting his executives to admit when things were not perfect was the basis of Mulally's turnaround. 'You can't manage a secret,' Mulally likes to say.[2] By forcing problems out into the open and making them everyone's problem, you get to faster, more effective solutions.

To fail well, be specific about what you're doing. What's the purpose? Is this an experiment? Are we learning here or demonstrating? Does everyone get it? Is compensation at all linked to success? If so, break the link. People do what they are rewarded for. Break the task down into small chunks, establish stage-gates at which you decided to stop or progress, and if at all possible, fail cheap and fail fast.

Having failed, it is important to put the failure in perspective. Is corrective action needed? Does someone need to be fired or a process overhauled? Or is it the kind of failure which is to be learned from? Did we fail well or poorly? And above all, as a manager, make

---

[2] 'The Happiest Man in Detroit', Keith Naughton, *Businessweek*, 3 February 2011

sure that those who failed well are properly and visibly rewarded so that your organisation understands what matters.

Managing success

In early 2011, Roger Federer's great tennis career appeared to be in decline. He had slipped from the number one ranking and would soon be turning 30. He was still the second ranked player in the world, but all that was ever said about him seemed to be negative. For any tennis player but Roger Federer, being No. 2 in the world would be a great achievement. Having been the best, being second best was seen by many as a failure. Fortunately, he showed a healthy perspective on the eve of that year's Australian Open. 'I think if you're world No. 1, everything that's good is great and everything that's not so good is OK. It never goes to really bad if you're the best', he said. 'And then if you drop to world No. 2, everything that was very good is only good now.'

He had identified a very common pattern, which applies just as much to business as to sports. By focusing excessively on outcomes, we end up misinterpreting the real causes of success and failure. A narrow win justifies everything which led up to it, while a narrow failure means you toss the plan away and start afresh. In success as in failure, maintaining the right perspective and focusing on the process rather than the outcome is vital.

> by focusing excessively on outcomes, we end up misinterpreting the real causes of success and failure

To help himself in 2011, Federer, already the winner of 16 Grand Slam tournaments, set about trying to improve his game. He hired a coach whom he had never worked with before, who did not carry the same assumptions about what worked and did not work for him, who could look at his game with fresh eyes.

But one thing he didn't change was his self-belief, the attribute he credits with turning him into the greatest player in the history of tennis. His skill and hard work had brought him close to the top. What made him dominant, he has often said, was his decision a few years into his career not to panic during games. No matter how things were going, he decided simply to hang in and hope for the best, rather than beating himself up or imagining defeat. You never know if an opponent is going to implode. But what you can control is your own self-belief and effort.

Roger Federer's success owes much to his ability to keep a cool, objective perspective on himself, so regardless of what others do or say, he can determine what is a success and what is a failure. A good manager will do the same, focusing on process and a proper perspective over outcomes and the ill-informed gossip of others.

The greatest risk of success is that it breeds overconfidence. After failures, people want to know the causes which led to the effects. If a plane crashes or the stock market plunges, inquiries are started and committees are formed to find out what happened and why. Not so with success. Amidst the celebrations, people forget to ask why they have succeeded as they have. Was it the concept, the execution, or pure dumb luck?

Unless we can attribute our successes to the right causes, we cannot learn from them and become less likely to be able to repeat them. Even worse, an eventual success might lead us to ignore how closely we flirted with catastrophe.

From the time of its founding in 2000, the American airline JetBlue enjoyed near universal acclaim as the airline which promised to 'bring humanity back to air travel'. It prided itself on treating customers better than its competitors, offering perks like seat-back television sets on domestic flights in America and comfortable headsets. It also boasted that it cancelled far fewer flights than its rivals due to bad weather. JetBlue preferred to get passengers on its planes quickly, pull the planes out fast and try to get ahead of bad weather.

But on Valentine's Day 2007 this approach backfired. An ice storm hit New York's JFK airport and hundreds of JetBlue passengers were stuck on the planes for 11 hours, in the cold, with foul-smelling lavatories. Customers were furious, JetBlue lost millions of dollars having to cancel many more flights and its reputation took a serious dent. A couple of days later, the CEO of JetBlue appeared on a late night comedy show in New York, but the host delayed his appearance on-stage, saying 'We'll make him wait for a change.'

Looking back, weather delays on JetBlue flights between 2003 and 2007 had tripled due to the airline's aggressive weather strategy. Even as the company had been piling up customer service awards, it had been increasing the risk that a fiasco would eventually occur. Success had blinded it to the growing risk of failure.

When disaster did strike, it created more of a problem for JetBlue than it might have for an airline with less respect from customers. With certain airlines, you expect poor service. JetBlue had demanded and received the trust of its customers and now it had let them down spectacularly. Fortunately, the airline responded well. Its CEO put himself at the forefront, apologising profusely and promising to revamp the way it compensated customers caught up in such travel nightmares, offering prompt refunds and vouchers in the case of excessive delays.

For any company whose reputation depends on service, there are two ways to blow yourself up: by being unreliable and by not resolving problems fairly. Having been unreliable, JetBlue did the right thing by going overboard on resolving the problems. Having dealt with the particular situation, it revamped its booking system and staff training and operations, and developed a team of corporate executives capable of swinging into action at JFK, whether handling bags or booking terminals, should any further problems arise.

Having mismanaged success, by lapping up the acclaim while letting its processes slip, JetBlue then had to do more to rescue itself from a failure than airlines which routinely disappoint their customers.

A third danger of success is that it closes our minds and changes our habits. Having succeeded, we abandon the very attitudes which enabled our success: curiosity, diligence, openness, a willingness to take calculated risk. Instead, we become complacent, our world shrinks to contain only other 'successful' people and we focus on hoarding and protecting what we have rather than seeking to expand or improve on it.

> having succeeded, we abandon the very attitudes which enabled our success

Albert Einstein did exactly this as he entered middle age. He was by this point the most famous scientist in the world. As a child, Einstein had been considered a mediocre intellect, and insolent at school. But as a teenager, he developed a fascination with science, which had nothing to do with what he was taught at school. He envisioned himself riding along at the speed of light, and fantasised about all kinds of objects whizzing through time and space. After attending university and failing to obtain an academic post, he took a job as a clerk in the Swiss patent office, and over the course of a few months in his mid-20s, he wrote five short papers which changed the history of science, challenging Newtonian physics and redrafting our view of space and time.

Suddenly, he was in hot academic demand and as his theories gained credibility and acceptance – he became one of the best known figures in the world, his shock of white hair, moustache and pipe completing the image of a mad but brilliant scientist. All the attention, however, conspired to make him a less inventive scientist. He complained that 'with fame, I become more and more stupid, which of course is a very common phenomenon'.[3] As he grew older, he found he could no longer think with the freedom

---

[3] *Einstein: His life and Universe*, Walter Isaacson, Simon & Schuster, 2007, p. 272

and verve of his youth. He dismissed new ideas by younger physicists, especially if they challenged his own. He loathed views which suggested there were uncertainties embedded in the universe, famously insisting that 'God does not play dice with the universe'. He even came to despise himself for what had happened to his own thinking, even while he became ever more famous, writing to a friend that 'the intellect gets crippled, but glittering renown is still draped around the calcified shell'.[4]

Between 1968 and 1972, a Californian entrepreneur, Stewart Brand, published a book called the *Whole Earth Catalog*, aimed at the counterculture of its time. It offered products ranging from clothing and books, to tools and seeds, to those who felt at odds with America's prevailing conservative culture and sought an alternative way of living, more creative, and more self-sustainable. It emphasised the importance of understanding the ecology in human life, an idea which has since become both fashionable and mainstream. It was an utterly original publication which inspired enormous devotion.

Three decades later, Apple's founder Steve Jobs called it one of the great inspirations of his life, especially the final edition published in 1974, which exhorted its readers to 'stay hungry, stay foolish'. That, said Jobs, was the best advice he could offer anyone.

It is the best advice a manager could heed for managing both failure and success.

---

[4] Ibid, p. 317

Top 10 tips for managing strategy

1   Understand the structure of your industry, as it will determine your profitability.

2   Important changes happen when you least expect it.

3   People will always criticise what challenges the status quo.

4   Don't be the last one left defending a dead strategy.

5   Strategies must be as fluid as the business environment demands.

6   Be as objective about your successes as about your failures.

7   Turning defensive almost never works.

8   Being open does.

9   Encourage experimentation while setting clear expectations about the rewards and punishments for various outcomes.

10 Set up noble failures to discover the right strategy.

Conclusion

I wrote at the start of this book that at the heart of management lay not rank, but responsibility. Great managers respond ably to whatever is demanded of them. They do not rely on their job title to persuade or force others to act. They rely on the respect which they have earned. They are kind and thoughtful not just when they need to be, but even when no one else is looking. They build up large reserves of credit with others, which they can draw upon to do difficult things.

Great managers have a keen sense of self. They know where they are strong and where they are weak, and they are unafraid to trust others to fill in the gaps.

But above all else, great managers get things done. They are constantly moving forward, learning from but not rueing the past. They understand what they can control in the present in order to create a better future. And they do not flinch from taking the wheel. They accept the task of leadership eagerly. They are willing to do what scares them, in the knowledge that it will make them better. They would rather do something and fail than do nothing for fear of falling short of perfection.

Management essentially falls into three categories: people, vision and operations. No one is more or less important than the other. If you can hire terrific

> management essentially falls into three categories: people, vision and operations

people, and have them work diligently at the details in order to achieve a great vision, then chances are you will be a world-class manager.

But within this framework are thousands of variations which depend on who you are. Every day in every form of media, managers discuss how they do what they do. The trick is finding patterns and habits which make sense to you.

Amy Astley, the editor of *Teen Vogue* in America, spent years training as a ballet dancer, which she says left her with high standards and a tendency not to sugar-coat problems: 'I really thrived with the high standards, and that's how I am now. I'm not too harsh on the people around me, but at the same time my standards are high. Not everybody can cut it.' This approach feeds into how she runs meetings. When she first became editor, she used to run big staff meetings with everyone in a conference room together. 'After I did that for six months or so, I realized that it quickly becomes like a high school cafeteria. You have your alpha girls. Two of them are best friends. They talk. They shut everybody else down. The other people don't say a peep – you'd think they've gone mute – and no new ideas are coming out.' She also found that following large meetings it was easy for people to evade responsibility.

So she stopped the big meetings and held more one-on-one meetings throughout the day. That way, she found it easier to give people clear directions, hear their point of view, assign responsibility and establish a clear course of action. Dealing with creative people, she also found they were more willing to take risks in private meetings and offer up provocative ideas without their colleagues listening in.[1]

Every industry and every organisation has its own peculiar features which call for different managerial practices. Christine

---

[1] 'Corner Office', interview with Amy Astley, *The New York Times*, 4 February 2012

Lagarde, the French lawyer and former finance minister who became head of the International Monetary Fund in 2011, has suggested that if there had been more women in finance, the global financial crash of 2008 might not have been so bad. After taking over at the IMF, she chose to consult a far wider group of advisers than her male predecessors had. 'My management style is more inclusive. Perhaps you can say that is because I am a woman – I do think that women tend to be more inclusive. I am very decisive when it comes to organising the team, but I do consult widely and hear many ideas before rushing in.'[2]

As the head of an international organisation, Lagarde has to pay close attention to politics. By contrast, H. Ross Perot, the Texan billionaire who made his fortune in technology and later ran twice as an independent candidate for the United States Presidency, liked to work by the principle of 'Ready, Fire, Aim'. Other companies, he said, spent too long aiming, searching for the target, preparing, only to miss their moment. Far better to get ready, take a shot and then recalibrate once you see how close you are. Only by trying lots of different things can you ever hope to succeed.

In his memoir, *Bloomberg by Bloomberg*, Michael Bloomberg wrote that in the early days of his business making and installing finance terminals for traders: 'We made mistakes, of course. Most of them were omissions we didn't think of when we initially wrote the software. We fixed them by doing it over and over, again and again. We do the same today. While our competitors are still sucking their thumbs trying to make the design perfect, we're already on prototype version #5. By the time our rivals are ready with wires and screws, we are on version #10. It gets back to planning versus acting: we act from day one; others plan how to plan – for months.'

Does this apply to your organisation and how you manage? If you do plan for months, is there a good reason for it? Or are you simply procrastinating, setting yourself up to be overtaken by the

---

[2] 'Power With Grace', interview with Gillian Tett, *Financial Times*, 9 December 2011

if you do plan for months, is there a good reason for it?

Bloombergs of this world? Are you doing what managers are supposed to do and taking responsibility? Or does your pattern of planning and action suggest you are shirking it?

It all starts with the small things, how you manage each minute of your day, how you talk to people, your common courtesies. From its founding in 2004, Facebook was a company built in the image of its founder, Mark Zuckerberg, highly intelligent and technically brilliant, but decidedly odd. Management was not the priority. Great programming was.

Zuckerberg, however, was smart enough to recognise the problem and seek out a solution. His investors introduced him to all kinds of executives, hoping one of them would click. Eventually Zuckerberg met Sheryl Sandberg, an executive at Google. They talked over a number of private dinners, discussing everything from their personal philosophies of life to the Internet advertising business, before Zuckerberg finally decided to offer her the job of Chief Operating Officer. 'There are people who are really good managers, people who can manage a big organization', he said. 'And then there are people who are very analytic or focussed on strategy. Those two types don't usually tend to be in the same person. I would put myself much more in the latter camp.'[3]

When Sandberg began work at Facebook, she walked up to hundreds of people at their desks, interrupted them and said 'Hi, I'm Sheryl Sandberg.' She set up meetings with Zuckerberg on Monday mornings and Friday afternoons and started dealing with what Zuckerberg called 'all that stuff in other companies I might have to do'. In other words, the management. Facebook still had many issues to resolve, not least how it might ever make money. Sandberg gathered senior executives for three-hour meetings in the early evening to thrash out these issues and reach agreement on

[3] 'A Woman's Place', Ken Auletta, *The New Yorker*, 11 July 2011

an advertising-based business model, until by 2010, Facebook was finally profitable and the number of its users had grown tenfold.

Great management can be a remarkable force in the world. But often it requires that you make the best of what others see as chores. Few people love meetings. But they are necessary to the social functioning of a business. So make the best of them. Become a master of meetings. Use them to inquire, persuade and motivate your team. Use them to develop your own skills and to convince others of your value.

> become a master of meetings

Similarly, keep expanding your network. Success is contagious. The most successful people tend to know lots of other successful people. There is plenty to complain about in modern organisations, plenty of managerial jargon, bureaucracy and time-wasting. Anyone can spend their day moaning about where they work. Great managers, though, do something about it, and surround themselves with others with a similar attitude. They do not let inertia and misery get the better of them. They either change what surrounds them, or they move into an environment where they can flourish, where they can be infected by success.

But perhaps the singular trait of great managers is this: they give a damn. They care about details, whether it is helping a young co-worker improve, or emptying an over-flowing trash can. If no one is sweeping the front step, they pick up a brush and sweep it. They care about how each memo reads and how each slide is designed. They draw up long to-do lists and complete everything on them.

They realise that impressions matter, that treating people decently matters, and that thinking through strategic issues matters. They are serious about their learning. They make sure that all their activities are integrated, just as any good company functions best when its divisions operate not as silos but as perfectly meshing gears, supporting and improving each other. They may experiment and fail, but they do this with intent, knowing that failing fast, often and intelligently is the surest route to eventual success.

All of this may sound like common sense. But it is rarely common practice. Which explains why management books are still written at all.

Select reading list for managers

The Four Steps to the Epiphany: Successful Strategies for Products that Win, Steven Gary Blank, Quad/Graphics, 2005

Out of the Crisis, W. Edwards Deming, MIT Press, 2000

ReWork: Change the Way You Work Forever, Jason Fried and David Heinemeier Hansson, Vermilion, 2010

Delivering Happiness: A Path to Profits, Passion and Purpose, Tony Hsieh, BusinessPlusUS, 2012

Reality Check: The Irreverent Guide to Outsmarting, Outmanaging, and Outmarketing Your Competition, Guy Kawasaki, Penguin, 2011

Against the Odds: An Autobiography, James Dyson, Texere Publishing, 2000

Transparency: How Leaders Create a Culture of Candor, Warren Bennis, Daniel Goleman and James O'Toole, Jossey Bass, 2008

Switch: How to Change Things when Change is Hard, Chip Heath and Dan Heath, Random House Business, 2011

Crossing the Chasm: Marketing and Selling Technology Products to Mainstream Customers, Geoffrey A. Moore, Capstone, 1998

Inside the Tornado: Strategies for Developing, Leveraging, and Surviving Hypergrowth Markets, Geoffrey A. Moore, HarperPaperbacks, 2004

The Innovator's Dilemma: When New Technologies Cause Great Firms to Fail, Clayton M. Christensen, Harvard Business School Press, 1997

The Innovator's Solution: Creating and Sustaining Successful Growth, Clayton M. Christensen, Harvard Business School Press, 2003

Influence: The Psychology of Persuasion, Robert Cialdini, HarperBusiness, 2007

Creating Modern Capitalism: How Entrepreneurs, Companies and Countries Triumphed in Three Industrial Revolutions, Thomas McCraw, Harvard University Press, 1998

Who: The A Method For Hiring, Geoff Smart and Randy Street, Ballantine Books, 2008

Good to Great: Why Some Companies Make the Leap ... And Others Don't, Jim Collins, Random House Business, 2004

Great by Choice: Uncertainty, Chaos and Luck – Why Some Thrive Despite Them All, Jim Collins and Morten T. Hansen, Random House Business, 2011

In the Plex: How Google Thinks, Works, and Shapes Our Lives, Steven Levy, Simon & Schuster, 2011

Tell to Win: Connect, Persuade and Triumph with the Hidden Power of Story, Peter Guber, Crown Business Books, 2011

Competitive Strategy: Techniques for Analyzing Industries and Competitors, Michael E. Porter, Free Press, 2004

In Search of Excellence: Lessons from America's Best-Run Companies, Robert H. Waterman and Tom Peter, Profile Books, 2004

The Little Big Things: 163 Ways to Pursue Excellence, Tom Peters, HarperBusiness, 2010

Leading Change, John P. Kotter, Harvard Business School Press, 1996

StrengthsFinder 2.0, Tom Rath, Gallup Press, 2007

Making Ideas Happen: Overcoming the Obstacles Between Vision and Reality, Scott Belsky, Penguin, 2011

Little Bets: How Breakthrough Ideas Emerge From Small Discoveries, Peter Sims, Random House Business, 2012

Wooden On Leadership, John Wooden, McGraw-Hill Professional, 2005

The Wisdom of Crowds: Why the Many Are Smarter Than the Few, James Surowiecki, Abacus, 2005

The Fifth Discipline: The Art and Practice of the Learning Organization, Peter M. Senge, Random House Business, 2006

Competing for the Future, Gary Hamel and C.K. Prahalad, Harvard Business School Press, 1996

The Practice of Management, Peter F. Drucker, Butterworth-Heinemann, 2007

The Progress Principle: Using Small Wins to Ignite Joy, Engagement, and Creativity at Work, Teresa Amabile and Steven Kramer, Harvard Business School Press, 2011

The Decision to Trust: How Leaders Create High-Trust Organizations, Robert F. Hurley, Jossey Bass, 2011

One Piece of Paper: The Simple Approach to Powerful, Personal Leadership, Mike Figliuolo, Jossey Bass, 2011

True North: Discover Your Authentic Leadership, Bill George, Jossey Bass, 2007

Getting Things Done: The Art of Stress-Free Productivity, David Allen, Piatkus, 2002

Ready For Anything: 52 Productivity Principles For Work and Life, David Allen, Piatkus, 2011

Appendix

The Financial Times articles in full

Nothing beats the exercise of judgment

By Phillip Delves Broughton

The phrase "paradigm shift" should be enough to send chills down any manager's spine. It is what consultants say when they don't know what else to recommend. Or economists, when all their predictions have just gone up in smoke. "What you need now, dear client, is a 'paradigm shift'. Here's my bill and I'll be off."

But since the failure of many financial institutions to predict or manage through the economic crisis, this is what many economists and business academics are calling for: a "paradigm shift" in how we think about the balance between human judgment and the efficiency of scale in running a profitable business.

In a recent piece in the Harvard Business Review, Amar Bhidé blamed the financial crisis "judgment deficit" on too many black box computer models and too few humans making decisions for themselves.

In this newspaper, the economist Joseph Stiglitz recently blamed markets and regulators for placing too much faith in the efficient markets hypothesis and assuming that market prices reflected fully all relevant information.

What is missing from this debate is the voice of the manager, the person who more than any economist or academic, understands this problem intuitively. Because in any business, large or small, financial crisis or none, this problem comes up every single day. Do you prefer to trust people or processes in running your business? In difficult moments, do you put your faith in the seemingly clean, dependable data or the executive who says she feels uneasy about the decision they are leading to?

A few years ago, economists were briefly fascinated by the distinction between hard and soft information. Hard information includes numbers, charts and empirical data. Soft information includes intuition, or personal judgments about people and situations. George Soros once said that he dumps positions when his lower back starts to ache. That's the soft signal that might support a hard judgment on the direction of the euro versus the dollar.

In hiring, a CV contains hard information about degrees obtained and jobs done. Personal references are the soft stuff, which help an employer distinguish between the blithering gasbag with blue chip degrees and the diligent genius with only a high school education. All big decisions require a balance of soft and hard information.

The other part of this problem is how you grow. Businesses requiring endless individual judgments are not nearly as scalable as those built on technology platforms. The reason banks came to depend on credit scores to make loans was that it simplified the process to the point where they could make more loans, faster, with what seemed like a satisfactory level of scrutiny.

The blow-ups of the past three years aside, it's hard to see this model fundamentally changing. Some may pine for the traditional bank manager tyrannising a local lending system, but the efficiency and profitability of scale lending is not going away.

Furthermore, it's not as though depending on soft information in finance is any protection against disaster. The success of micro-lending in the developing world may seem to justify extending credit based on soft information, the observation that people without any financial history will work hard to fulfil their obligations to their families and communities.

But then Bernie Madoff's scam was a victory of soft over hard information. The whispered remark in Palm Beach, "this Madoff's a genius", was valued more than any proper look at what Madoff was doing.

The slow growth of person-to-person lending may in part be because most of us still value the impersonal lending processes of large institutions.

Bo Burlingham's excellent book *Small Giants – Companies that choose to be great instead of big* – describes several US companies that faced similar challenges to the ones that economists are now debating. Given the opportunity to become bigger, do you seize it? Or is there something magical about staying small? What are the pitfalls of size? At what point does a manager go from being a manager of people to an implementer of organisational processes? And what gets lost if that happens?

I know the chief executive of a Midwestern company with 90 employees who believes firmly that going beyond that would change the nature of the company for the worse. He frets that his employees would lose their sense of purpose, the sense that their work and the decisions they make matter. It means passing up opportunities to scale what he does, but he believes that preserving the human dimension of his company is worth it.

This is not to say there is virtue in staying small. But rather that for the right manager and company, there is value – just as there is value for others in being large. It comes down to what economists struggle to model and managers grapple with all day: judgment. No paradigm shift required.

FT

Source: Delves Broughton, P., 'Nothing beats the exercise of judgement', *The Financial Times*, 6 September 2010.

The Hollywood boss is no work of fiction

By Phillip Delves Broughton

In *Money Never Sleeps*, the just released sequel to *Wall Street*, Gordon Gekko tells us that "idealism kills deals". It is the most pungent line in the film, and a bracing rejoinder to anyone who argues that business is about "doing well by doing good". In fact, the whole film, like the original, is a perverse homage to appalling behaviour.

But whereas Gekko is fictional, Mark Zuckerberg, the founder of Facebook, is the all-too-real central character in *The Social Network*, the other business world blockbuster of the autumn. Mr Zuckerberg is not just portrayed as ambitious, a reasonable trait in the founder of a start-up, but also as vengeful, vicious, duplicitous and devoid of even the most basic social skills.

Interviewed by Oprah Winfrey last week, Mr Zuckerberg said of the film: "A lot of it is fiction, but even the film-makers will say that. They're building a good story. This is my life, I know it's not that dramatic. The last six years have been a lot of coding and focus and hard work. But maybe it will be fun to remember it as partying and all this crazy drama."

It is a story we have seen before among the technology greats of the past 30 years. The young Bill Gates, by most accounts, was a similar kind of nightmare, screaming at his staff and elbowing aggressively past rivals as he built Microsoft.

When he founded Apple, Steve Jobs was said to push his developers to work ungodly hours and to treat both colleagues and competitors with contempt.

And yet how much of this makes it into the management books? Where is the guru who tells us that the way to get the most out of an organisation is to ratchet up the pressure until everyone is desperate and frazzled? And then to run psychological rings round them?

Why is it left to Hollywood to tell us what we already know, that those who succeed in business are not always the most likable people? That to succeed on the epic scale of a Zuckerberg, Gates or Gekko, may require some deeply unpalatable traits?

I once heard Steve Schwarzman, the chief executive of the Blackstone Group, talk about the importance of competitiveness in his business. To win in private equity, you really have to hustle. Fair enough.

But then came the incident last month, when he compared President Barack Obama's threats to raise taxes on private equity investments to "when Hitler invaded Poland in 1939". He has since apologised but when a multibillionaire testily compares a tax rise to the second world war, that spirit of competitiveness has evidently gone too far.

But what is the ordinary manager to make of it all? There you sit in a negotiation seminar learning about creating "win-win" situations, while part of you suspects that, as one corporate lawyer once put it to me, "the only win-win situation is one where the same person wins twice".

There you are downloading the latest rules on diversity and sexual harassment, while Mr Zuckerberg, whose last venture before Facebook was a website that invited users to rank female students at Harvard by physical attractiveness, rockets past towards billions.

In *Hardball: Are Your Playing to Play or Playing to Win?*, one of the few books to address this issue of business's dark side, George Stalk and Rob Lachenauer, two consultants at Boston Consulting Group, wrote: "Winners in business play rough and don't apologise." They argued that hardball is not about breaking the law or cheating, but about relentless competition, bordering on brutality, and absolute clarity of purpose. It is certainly not about "people skills".

The Hardball way lists five "fundamental behaviours of winning": "focus relentlessly on competitive advantage"; "strive for extreme competitive advantage", don't be happy just being better at something, but try to be much, much better; "avoid attacking directly", because unless you have overwhelming force, you are better off being sneaky; "exploit people's will to win", by motivating them to become slavering, hyper-competitive beasts; and "know the caution zone", play to the edges of the pitch, but not beyond.

They then list five strategies to be deployed in "bursts of ruthless intensity". These are: "devastate rivals' profit sanctuaries"; "plagiarise with pride"; "deceive the competition"; "unleash massive and overwhelming force" once you have it; and "raise competitors' costs", the final turn of the ratchet after you have destroyed their profits, copied, tricked and beaten them unconscious.

"Hardball is tough, not sadistic," they write. "Yes, you want rivals to squirm, but not so visibly that you are viewed as a bully. In fact, you want the people in your world – the same ones you demand straight answers from – to cheer you on. And many of them will, as they share the riches your strategies generate."

Fail at hardball, or its more extreme derivations, and you may not even have the consolation of having fought a decent fight. But succeed, and you will have all the resources in the world to buy your way to redemption – however Hollywood depicts you.

When to turn a blind eye to the facts

By Phillip Delves Broughton

"The good news from the Gulf of Mexico is that the worst predictions of environmental disaster after the Deepwater Horizon oil rig exploded are unlikely to be fulfilled. It's still awful, but not as awful as first feared. But when you think back to the worst days, as BP struggled to cap the well against a cacophony of abuse, there were two kinds of decision making on display.

For the men and women fighting to stop the leak, there were the messy, practical challenges to be met, and decisions to be made based on the evidence. And then there were those who made the decision early to pound away at this latest example of "Big Oil" gone wild.

President Barack Obama was caught between the two, trying to make decisions based on the complex set of facts, while others claimed to know exactly what decisions should be made, and compiled the evidence accordingly.

Businesses are often caught in the same trap. Ideally, you want to base your decisions on sound evidence. But often, managers make a decision then rustle up the evidence to support it. As Peter Tingling and Michael Brydon of Simon Fraser University wrote recently in the MIT Sloan Managment Review, it is the difference between evidence-based decision making and its ugly sibling, decision-based evidence making.

British schoolchildren are taught the story of Lord Nelson at the Battle of Copenhagen. When told that his commander was signalling for him to retreat, Nelson raised a telescope to his blind eye and said: "I really do not see the signal."

Within a few hours, the Danish fleet was defeated. He had made the decision to fight and moulded the evidence to fit. "If you get the outcome you want, then everything is fine," says Prof Tingling.

But in a world that venerates data-driven decision making, whether in financial services or sports management, managers are often loath to admit that they still take the Nelson approach to make the decision first and find the evidence later.

Profs Tingling and Brydon found that evidence is used by managers in three different ways: to make; inform; or support a decision. If it is used to make a decision, it means the decision arises directly from the evidence. If it is used to inform a decision, evidence is mixed in with intuition or bargaining to lead to a decision. If it is used to support a decision, it means the evidence is simply a means to justify a decision already made. They also found that evidence is often shaped by subordinates to meet what they perceive to be the expectations of their bosses.

There are two dangers to letting decisions trump evidence. The first is when decision making is simply ill-informed. Ideally, a decision that contradicts the evidence is an inspired hunch, formed by experience, like Nelson's. In the worst case, it is the product of ignorant bias.

The second danger is that once your employees know that you, as a manager, are more interested in finding evidence to fit your conclusions rather than seeking out truth, it infects a company with demoralising and destructive cynicism.

When Herman Miller designed the Aeron chair, consumer focus groups were hostile. But the company ignored them and went ahead with production anyway. The chair was a huge hit. The company was capable of taking evidence and successfully ignoring it.

In other companies, however, the cult of data-driven decision making leaves so little room for personal beliefs that people just tailor evidence to fit pre-made decisions.

At Ford in the 1950s, Robert McNamara, then chief executive, demanded data on everything. Interns would cut up newspapers and paste them into binders so executives could point to the voluminous research that went into each decision.

Vince Kaminski, who led Enron's research division, has spoken of the frustrations of having 50 highly skilled mathematicians picking apart Enron's risky deals only to be ignored by executives who prized volume above all else.

So what is a manager to do? How do you encourage the use of data, while leaving room for the occasional inspired decision? One solution is to be more flexible in how you categorise decisions. Not all will require the same degree of evidence.

Another is to weigh the costs of gathering evidence. Is it always worth it? If not, don't fudge it for appearance's sake. Admit that you are trusting your well-honed instincts. This is especially true for those within your company. Sometimes you will have to come up with tendentious evidence for an external audience, which demands at least a charade of evidence. But don't ever pretend for those inside. They will know better and punish the slightest deceit either now or well into the future."

Source: Delves Broughton, P., 'When to turn a blind eye to the facts', *The Financial Times*, 20 September 2010.

Break the model on employee behaviour

By Phillip Delves Broughton

If ever there were a moment for companies to be experimenting with how they organise and motivate their employees, now would seem to be it. Businesses are being yanked in every direction by the forces of recession, emerging markets and new technology. Psychologists and economists are collaborating as never before to expand the field of behavioural economics, to tell us why we behave the way we do when it comes to work and money.

So why are more companies not using the crisis to rethink how they manage their people? Why are they so much more innovative when it comes to jiggering with their balance sheet or product line than human resources?

It is a question that is dumbfounding Dan Ariely, a professor of behavioural economics at Duke University and author of two books, *Predictably Irrational* and *The Upside of Irrationality*. Prof Ariely is one of management's most widely cited behavioural economists, and he told me that while companies harried him for insights into customer behaviour, they were loath to try out anything new on their employees. "There is no worse place to try to do experiments than human resources," he said. "The first thing on their mind when they hear the word 'experiment' is lawsuits."

➡

Some of Prof Ariely's most interesting research has been in the area of compensation. He has concluded, for example, that large bonuses have little effect on the performance of bankers. He suggests that banks would be better off firing all but their most talented employees and hiring thousands of new workers with none of the salary and bonus expectations of the old ones. They would be able to do the same work for much less money, unburdened by outlandish expectations. I would love to hear Jamie Dimon and Lloyd Blankfein debate that one.

Prof Ariely argues that financial rewards are only one piece of a complex web of motivations which affect each of us differently. These include a sense of purpose, status, altruism, ego and control, all of which a clever manager should take into account. And yet how many do this in anything but the most informal way?

"I went to a lot of companies and said, 'Let's do studies of bonuses,'" he says. "One hundred per cent of the time, people would tell us that bonus season is so miserable, they didn't want to prolong the agony by studying it any further – even though we know that productivity goes down during bonus season and that bonuses are not the most efficient motivator."

He added that "the biggest curse in compensation are compensation consulting firms" that do nothing but benchmark compensation against companies, which may or may not be useful comparisons. "They know nothing about the science," says Prof Ariely. "They're just perpetuating the misery."

It may be that companies don't have Prof Ariely's urgency. Managers who have survived the recession intact are probably feeling confident in their existing model. Now may not seem the time to go redrafting the rewards structure and instituting flexi-time for all.

Prof Ariely says he still receives plenty of calls from start-ups, brimming with enthusiasm for new organisational forms. They crave new ideas about compensation and how to improve employee morale and creativity. They are eager to use unconventional methods to motivate individuals who spend their days working away from the main office on unusual schedules, and may only ever see parts rather than the whole of a business.

But once these companies reach any kind of scale, the experimental mindset hardens into a procedural one. The enthusiasm to get the most out of every individual becomes a desire to settle on a one-size-fits-all motivational template, regardless of the irrational behaviours it might cause.

The only way Prof Ariely has found through this inertia is to get the chief executive on side. He began working with Scott Cook of Intuit, the financial software company, on experiments to understand the behaviour of his customers. Why, for example, do people pay down their smallest loans before those that carry the highest interest rates? He suggested creating a software tool to help customers behave more rationally.

But now he says his behavioural economics research is seeping into Intuit's internal organisation. Instead of offering purely financial incentives for great work, Intuit now offers high-performing employees half a year's sabbatical.

Mr Cook is also encouraging a culture of experimentation, telling employees that a failed experiment is no failure if it produces evidence. This is vital to employees' feelings of control.

Innovative management that takes the complexity of human behaviour into account can be a competitive advantage – especially now, when so few are ready to practice it.

 Source: Delves Broughton, P., 'Break the model on employee behaviour', *The Financial Times*, 4 October 2010.

The winning tactic of cultural continuity

By Phillip Delves Broughton

"Assuming that Liverpool Football Club is sold to John Henry and his team from New England Sports Ventures, and that current owners, Tom Hicks and George Gillett quietly walk away from the club they have grievously mismanaged, what then? How does an American group with experience in baseball, ice hockey, hedge funds and sitcoms manage a club like Liverpool?

I grew up in Northampton, an English town with a lamentable football team. Supporting the Cobblers was a weekly dose of woe. But peering up from the bowels of the Fourth Division as it was then, there was always Liverpool to watch. It experienced the highest highs – European Cups and a record number of domestic championships – and the lowest lows – hooliganism and the Heysel and Hillsborough stadium disasters in which scores of fans lost their lives. One of the club's great managers, Bill Shankly, summed up life at Liverpool when he said "some people think football is a matter of life and death. I assure you, it's much more serious than that."

And then, last month, the impossible happened. My poor, shabby Cobblers, still a minnow of the sport, confronted Liverpool and beat them. For an investor such as Mr Henry, it must have confirmed that here was one of the great turnround opportunities in sport.

He comes at Liverpool's problem with an astonishing bench. His fellow investors are Jeffrey Vinik, former manager of Fidelity's gargantuan Magellan Fund turned successful hedge fund manager; Michael Gordon, Mr Vinik's former partner; David Ginsberg, one of Mr Henry's former fund managers, and Tom Werner, the producer of television mega-series such as *The Cosby Show* and *Roseanne*. Mr Henry can also deploy Michael Porter, his strategy adviser at the Boston Red Sox and the world's most influential business academic.

Applying his widely taught Five Forces analysis to measure the attractiveness of English football, Prof Porter would find that its competitive rivalry is intense, measured week after week by results on the pitch as well as on income statements. The threat of new entrants is low, as the same handful of clubs tend to dominate European football year after year. The threat of substitutes is equally small, as football fans are not easily swayed to other sports. The bargaining power of customers is low as fans rarely switch allegiance, and sponsors and broadcasters are desperate to tap into the sport's popularity.

Unfortunately, the bargaining power of suppliers, the players, is where football's economic attractiveness breaks down. Wage inflation has made it hard for even the most successful clubs to turn a large profit. As Deloitte said in its latest Review on Football Finance: "We [are] seeing a continuing shift from a sustainable 'not for profit' model towards one with potentially calamitous, consistent and significant lossmaking characteristics."

Three business models have surfaced in English football in recent years.

The open cheque book model at Chelsea and Manchester City, where a multibillionaire owner decides to spend whatever it takes to buy success. The leveraged buy-out model, at Manchester United and Liverpool, where foreign owners hobble their clubs with debt and find themselves loathed by fans. And finally the Arsenal model, where a steady management focuses on cash flow from player transfers and property, as well as the usual tickets, merchandise and broadcast rights, and remains competitive without straining to win at all costs.

➡

Mr Henry could get Liverpool for a bargain price. The club still has devoted fans and extraordinary players. But he does not have the billions of Roman Abramovich at Chelsea and, after Liverpool's near bankruptcy, is unlikely to find fresh lines of easy credit. As another American buying a British team, his leash with the fans will be short.

His first move, then, should be to show he is a worthy owner of the club by reviving its unique management system. From the 1960s to the 1990s, Liverpool's glory years, the heart of this system was "the boot room". Conjuring up images of muddy tracksuits and stewing tea, it was the room where managers, coaches and senior players would gather and talk. After matches, opposing managers were invited as well. The boot room was where winning habits were set and future managers trained. It created cultural continuity, and just as at General Electric, Liverpool's boot room was about promoting from within.

But in the late 1990s, after some mediocre years, Liverpool abandoned the boot room. It hired outside managers who failed to restore the club's edge. If Mr Henry's first act were to restore the boot room, it would show respect for Liverpool's traditions, the fans would love it, and it would buy him time while he ponders what to do with his cheque book."

 Source: Delves Broughton, P., 'The winning tactic of cultural continuity',
The Financial Times, 11 October 2010.
© The Financial Times Limited 2010. All rights reserved.

A new route from idea to reality

By Philip Delves Broughton

Bob Ianucci, the former chief technology officer at Nokia, used to give a talk about the evolutionary patterns in the technology industry called "I've seen this movie before". In it he described how every big technological change, from mainframes to minicomputers to PCs, had followed the same path.

PCs, for example, began with several companies – Apple, Commodore, Wang and others – offering their own incompatible hardware and software. Then a standard platform emerged in IBM. Compatible hardware followed – Dell, Hewlett-Packard, Intel and Compaq – before the value shifted to software – Microsoft – and finally to services and companies such as IBM, EDS and Oracle.

This pattern appears to be unfolding again in mobile phone technology. First, we had an array of separate systems. Now a platform war is being waged, most aggressively between Google's Android and Apple's iPhone operating systems.

Last month, Steve Jobs lashed into Android saying "we think Android is very, very fragmented and getting more fragmented by the day". Nokia is pitching in with new phones powered by its revamped Symbian OS, and Research in Motion's BlackBerry OS is another potent rival.

But already we are seeing hardware makers and the developers of software and mobile services circling this piranha tank, trying to decide which platforms will thrive or die, and which to invest in.

The difference between the history of mobile technology and PCs is the pace of the change. Product development cycles are now faster than traditional corporate innovation structures seem able to cope with. And while some, such as Apple and Google, seem comfortable with the speed of change, others such as Nokia and RIM are criticised for playing innovation catch-up with the Silicon Valley swells.

"There are so many opportunities, technologies and ideas, all of which are easily accessible," says Roberto Verganti, professor of management of innovation at Politecnico di Milano. "So, the key challenge for companies is not having the ideas, but making sense of them and having a vision. The companies that are most successful are the ones that understand the meaning behind the technology."

As a percentage of revenue, Nokia spent four times as much as Apple on research and development last year, and yet it has no market-changing products to show for it. Companies that try to compete on features or performance, Prof Verganti says, only briefly have an edge before everyone else catches up.

Moreover, consumers are not that interested in the features that might excite an internal research lab. When RIM came up with the BlackBerry, it perceived that what many users most wanted from their phones was e-mail, and they could happily do without the rest of the OS software. Apple was not the first to make an MP3 player, but the good-looking iPod combined with iTunes removed the whiff of illegality around music downloads. Apple was similarly the first to make sense of touchscreen technology with its iPhone. It was more than a gimmick: it changed how people thought of their phones.

Eric von Hippel, professor of technological innovation at the MIT Sloan School of Management, says a technology company should divide its research and innovation tasks "into those it can solve internally and those that can most effectively be solved outside". The ones that can be solved within are "dimension-of-merit" improvements such as better screen resolution, ergonomics or interface design. Those that must be solved outside are those that involve new customer needs. In 2007, for example, when Apple first released the iPhone, thousands of users decided to "jail-break" the software in order to customise it. Prof von Hippel says this prompted Steve Jobs to release a software developer kit, which in turn led to the explosion of the App Store. Apple was forced by outside events to open up its platform, although it remains controlled.

"Senior managers have to recognise that the innovation system has to be fundamentally reworked," says Prof von Hippel. "It's not a matter of tweaking. There is a fundamental new paradigm out there." This new model was created by falling design and communication costs, which have enabled more people to be part of the process. Prof von Hippel says managers need to venture out to the leading edges of their market and engage with users. He calls it "democratising innovation".

Prof Verganti agrees, saying technology companies must listen to "interpreters" – individuals inside and outside the company capable of understanding cultural and social forces beyond the immediate world of technology. These are not traditional market researchers, but people from other industries and professions who look at what you are doing with fresh eyes.

Few companies could use an innovation boost more than Nokia. Ari Hakkarainen, a former marketing executive at Nokia, says the company remains a serious business, selling more than 400m phones, from high- to low-end devices depending on the market. In order to avoid becoming just a low-cost competitor, however, it is trying pull off the trick of innovating without upsetting existing customers and profitable lines.

In September, the company replaced Olli-Pekka Kallasvuo, its chief executive, with Stephen Elop from Microsoft. While Mr Elop finds his feet, Nokia lacks a powerful CEO, in the mould of Mr Jobs or RIM's Mike Lazaridis, who can establish a vision and impose it on an organisation. "You need a strong leader to make these kinds of innovations become reality," Mr Hakkarainen says.

There is hope. With Apple entrenched at the high end of the mobile phone market, both Mr Hakkarainen and Prof von Hippel see a huge opportunity for Nokia innovating in emerging markets.

Andrew Hargadon, a professor of technology management at the UC Davis Graduate School of Management, worked at Apple in the early 1990s. "We were reinventing the wheel left and right," he says. "But to do that we built a factory that could never be profitable."

When Mr Jobs returned in 1996, says Prof Hargadon: "Apple chose not to be a technological leader. It said we're going to take technologies that are already out there and build a more seamlessly integrated network around that."

What Apple does, he says, "is identify a vision, then assemble the right team to pull that off". Such focus on a handful of products and highly tailored processes in marketing and distribution, such as the Apple Stores, is a contrast to companies where "top managers want to to be focused on new business units, but don't have time, yet refuse to cede authority" – so they end up "with one foot on the dock, one foot in the boat".

Rather than reorganising existing assets to try to come up with a new vision, Prof Hargadon says, technology companies must have the vision and then assemble the assets needed from outside and inside in order to make it real.

RIM's unveiling of its iPad rival, the Playbook, he says, is worrying. "I love RIM's products, which stay true to the original vision and do exactly what they do really well. To the extent they're trying to turn that hedgehog into a fox, they risk losing it."

Leadership is not just for the extroverts

By Phillip Delves Broughton

One of the paradoxes of leadership is that the people who most want to lead are often the last people we would want given the responsibility. The pushy hack, the selfish careerist and the ruthless opportunist are just some of the unpleasant types who tend to force their way to the top. They thrive in hyper-competitive environments. Decent people, who might actually make better leaders, seem to have a harder time scrambling upwards. They may have exactly what it takes to lead, but lack what it takes to get the chance.

My smell test for business leaders is if they talk about the importance of humility. The moment the word leaves their mouth, I assume they are the worst kind of corporate hypocrite, on the very simple basis that truly humble people don't boast about being humble.

One way academics have sought to categorise the character traits required to succeed has been to divide us into extroverts and introverts, and much research has found that it is the extroverts who do best.

Extroverts like to be the centre of attention, seek status and approval and talk a lot in social settings. They are good at motivating employees and leading change. Consequently, they earn more and get more promotions. Larry Ellison of Oracle and Jamie Dimon of JPMorgan Chase are prominent extrovert leaders, thrusting themselves forward in their company's interests.

So what hope is there for introverts? Are they simply to bask in the sun of the extroverts? Or can they lead too? Absolutely, say Adam Grant, Francesca Gino and David Hoffman, business school professors and authors of an intriguing new paper, "Reversing the Extroverted Leadership Advantage: The Role of Employee Proactivity", published in the Academy of Management Journal. They argue that one key variable has been underestimated in the argument over which character-type does best in business. And that is the degree to which a manager's employees are proactive.

If employees are passive, they found, an extrovert thrives by giving a clear lead. If employees are more proactive, the introvert does better because he actually listens and incorporates their advice into his decision-making.

What is novel here is that up to now, the advice for introverts in business has generally been to be more extroverted, to follow the old salesman's mantra, "act enthusiastic to be enthusiastic". But many forced grins later, is this really the best way for them to succeed?

It is clearly not necessary to be the life and soul of a party in order to run a great business. Bill Gates, Steve Jobs and Mark Zuckerberg are neither natural glad-handers nor extroverts, but all have the bullheadedness and genius that drags others along. Anna Wintour at Vogue and Giorgio Armani are frosty characters who are nonetheless accomplished managers in a highly creative industry. Sir Richard Branson has turned himself into an extrovert for the public but is said to be an introvert in private.

The academics drew on two sets of data. The first was from a chain of pizza restaurants, where they analysed financial performance and the nature of the managers and employees. The second came from a lab experiment, where they asked people to act either extroverted or introverted in managing a group folding T-shirts. The evidence showed that a proactive group either butted heads or felt underappreciated working for an extrovert leader and performed better under an introvert. The passive groups worked best for an extrovert and felt lost under an introvert.

Prof Grant told me that introverts do especially well at engineering and accounting companies, which tend to emphasise technical skills over personality. But other industries, especially those "with a lot of velocity and environmental turbulence", could benefit from hiring, valuing and promoting more introverts.

Extrovert leaders might succeed in these environments, but it's rather like putting all your money on a single number on the roulette wheel. Far better to have an introvert leader ready to absorb a lot of input in order to discover the best processes or business models.

To get to be leaders, introverts must still prove themselves terrific individual contributors. Without the noise and flash of the extrovert, they will have to find subtler ways to show they can lead. But once in a leadership or managerial position, they no longer need to worry about loosening up at parties and becoming more extroverted.

Instead, they can succeed by surrounding themselves with proactive employees, and giving them the autonomy and responsibility they require to perform at their best. They can focus on encouraging behaviour that complements their existing style rather than trying to acquire an awkward new one.

Hedge fund lessons on letting stars shine

By Phillip Delves Broughton

Saying you admire hedge funds, beyond some very narrow circles, makes you immediately unpopular. What's to like about those economic vandals, smashing and grabbing their way to billions while the rest of the world wades through the treacle of post-crisis recovery?

Yet last week, assets managed by hedge funds topped $2,000bn, a record. For all the venom directed their way, they continue to thrive, and it is worth considering how these vital players in our economic life are managed. Is there some management system beyond good asset selection, nimble trading and an eye-watering compensation system that makes hedge funds go?

Ray Dalio, founder of Bridgewater, a $90bn fund with 1,000 employees, is one of a few hedge fund titans to have written a theory of management. Called "Principles", it reads like a curious mating of Ayn Rand and the Dalai Lama, with a dash of sharp-elbowed MBA. Mr Dalio's company is 35 years old but he founded it just two years out of business school. The key theme of "Principles" is the importance of truth, "radical truth" and "radical transparency", in an organisation designed to foster and profit from original investment ideas. There must be truth around analysis, character, trust and, of course, compensation. As Mr Dalio writes, "pursuing self-interest in harmony with the laws of the universe and contributing to evolution is universally rewarded", even when that pursuit involves operating "like a hyena attacking the wildebeest".

More Money Than God, Sebastian Mallaby's superb history of hedge funds, contains stories of management lunacy that make Mr Dalio's jungle metaphors seem tame. Michael Steinhardt, one of the greatest traders of the 1970s and 1980s, realised his temper was creating dysfunction within his company. He allowed a psychiatrist to talk to his employees. The psychiatrist kept hearing phrases such as "battered children", "random violence" and "rage disorder". Mr Steinhardt eventually lost his temper with the shrink and threw him out.

Julian Robertson, founder of Tiger, would try to bond analysts by leading them on macho adventures into the mountains.

Hedge funds are run more like old-school Hollywood studios than financial institutions. They exist to support one or perhaps a handful of supposed investment geniuses – the talent. When the people who manage them are also the ones making the nerve-jangling investment decisions, it makes for a combustible atmosphere. Financial incentives, which can be colossal, tend to govern everything. Performance is measured in fractions of a basis point rather than 360-degree review sessions. Talent is rewarded lavishly and failure punished swiftly.

Lynn Stratton, a law professor at UCLA, wrote recently in the Harvard Business Review that hedge funds are "criminogenic" environments. She argues that hedge fund managers give the impression that all that matters is maximising returns, ethics be damned, and that financial crimes are victimless. Well, some of them maybe. But they stand at the end of a long line of far better-known companies that have wreaked more damage with similar cultures. Subprime mortgage lenders and those who recklessly securitised bad loans spring to mind.

Aside from enriching their best managers, hedge funds have earned billions for pension plans and endowments over the years, providing diversification where more ordinary financial institutions could not. The best have proved enduring, profitable, stable and innovative.

Their most important management feature is the ability to manage billions of dollars with just a few people. No hedge fund manager sets out to build the next JPMorgan Chase or Fidelity. Paulson & Co, run by John Paulson, employs 115 people to manage about $35bn in assets, or $304m per employee. Fidelity, the mutual fund and financial services group, by contrast, manages $3,500bn with 37,000 employees, or $94m per employee. Mr Paulson is liberated by the size of his organisation to do what he does best – punt on the collapse of the housing market or the rise in the price of gold.

Another vital piece of hedge fund management is requiring employees to keep their money in the company. About 40 per cent of Paulson & Co's assets under management belong to the partners and employees. Any investor knows the managers have skin in the game.

Hedge funds also tend to pay their support staff well. Receptionists, secretaries and chefs are handsomely rewarded for making the lives of the investors and analysts easier. It cuts to this central management challenge of managing the talent, these difficult, gifted people who generate outsized returns. You do that by creating an environment for them to focus on what it is they do extraordinarily well.

Bureaucratic efficiency, few distractions and great coffee will take you a long way.

Source: Delves Broughton, P., 'Hedge fund lessons on letting stars shine', *The Financial Times*, 25 April 2011.

Joined-up thinking

By Phillip Delves Broughton

There is no more powerful belief in business than the one that vigorous competition leads to success. It is embedded in economic and management theories, investment models and motivational speeches and, for some companies, is part of how they do business.

But a persuasive new set of theories is emerging, arguing that co-operation trumps competition. The fittest do not survive merely by outrunning their rivals. Rather, they win by finding ways to work together, by building the systems of trust and co-operation that allow groups to flourish.

This may be hard for many business people to swallow, given how embedded their competitive instincts have become. But in their new book *Super Cooperators*, Martin Nowak, a Harvard professor of biology and mathematics, and Roger Highfield, editor of the New Scientist magazine, argue that the winners in life are those who resist the temptation to escalate conflicts. The losers punish others and perish as a result.

Their argument rests on Prof Nowak's study of evolutionary principles which develop Charles Darwin's famous views. Humans are "supercooperators", they say, because we manifest selfless behaviour that results from natural selection. We advance as a species not by beating each other, but rather by trusting each other and working together. This explains why ants build their colonies and humans build cities.

Applied to business, Prof Nowak says "the ultimate lesson is that it is co-operation, not competition, that underpins innovation. To spur creativity, and to encourage people to come up with original ideas, you need to use the lure of the carrot, not fear of the stick ... Without co-operation, there can be neither construction nor complexity."

Co-operation in business, however, can take many forms. Employees within a single organisation might co-operate to achieve shared goals. Or companies can co-operate with each other to dominate a market. And co-operation and competition are often not antithetical, but can be mutually supporting. By co-operating, for example, a company's employees might trounce their competitor. "If at one bank, everyone is cut-throat, and at another everyone is collaborating, over time the collaborators will win," says Prof Nowak.

The Harvard Business School academics Clay Christensen, Matt Marx and Howard Stevenson have written that there are various ways to persuade people within an organisation to set aside their competitive instincts and co-operate. The key for a manager is to gauge how strongly his employees agree on where to go and the means of getting there. Then, he can use one of four sets of tools to get them to collaborate: power, management, leadership or culture.

The four tools range from highly aggressive to a gentle chivvying along and the management challenge is to know when to use which device. Power tools such as coercion and threats are used when employees agree on neither goals nor means. Management tools, such as training and measurement, work when employees agree on the goal but not on how to get there. Leadership tools, such as speeches and big vision statements, work to elicit co-operation in a well-functioning organisation towards a new goal. Culture tools, such as emphasising tradition and employee involvement, are the softest of all and work in companies capable of managing themselves.

An extreme example of power leadership was Jamie Dimon, chief executive of JPMorgan Chase, when he led the company's merger with Bank One. Profs Christensen, Marx and Stevenson write that during the merger, Mr Dimon cut executive salaries by as much as 50 per cent, threatened branch managers with the sack if they failed to meet quota, and warned the IT division that if they didn't choose a single platform for the merged businesses' IT within six weeks, he would pick one himself.

Starbucks' chief executive Howard Schultz used both power and leadership tools when he returned to the company he founded as chief executive in 2008. He employed the first when he closed stores and fired thousands of employees. Once he had got the company back into shape, he then wrote *Onward: How Starbucks Fought For its Life Without Losing its Soul* to explain himself and act as a leadership tool to rally his battered troops.

The trick for executives is to get the balance right. It takes a particular blend of co-operation and competition to rise to the top of a large organisation. Even the most competitive individual requires the support of others to succeed. But co-operate too much, and you risk being taken advantage of by others.

Mark Weber of the University of Waterloo and J. Keith Murnighan of Northwestern University have written that the people who always volunteer and rally teams to overcome problems are invaluable to companies, but are treated as suckers for not pursuing their own interests. In larger companies, says Prof Murnighan, "it's harder now for consistent co-operators to benefit from their actions. The consistent co-operator gets burnt once, and it takes a strong character to come back from that."

As companies change more quickly and employees come and go with greater frequency, it is harder than ever to reap the long-term rewards of collaboration. Everyone is operating on a shorter time horizon, which leads to more self-interested behaviour.

Bruce Henderson, founder of the Boston Consulting Group, wrote a well-known article in 1967 titled Brinkmanship in Business, which he said could equally be titled "How to Succeed in Business by Being Unreasonable". He wrote that to compete effectively, it was necessary to appear to be co-operating while in fact ensuring you get your own way. He compared business to international relations during peace time, when countries compete ferociously but exercise restraint to avoid war. "The goal of the hottest economic war," he wrote, "is an agreement for coexistence, not annihilation."

Some of the world's biggest industries exhibit just these alternating patterns of competition and co-operation. Coca-Cola and Pepsi may seem in constant battle, but their duopoly allows them to limit market access by smaller rivals and maintain pricing. Microsoft and Intel may have made billions from their near dominance in personal computing, but it has not stopped them fighting over how to divide up the profits. They co-operate to create value, but compete to appropriate it.

Among venture capitalists and technology companies, the term "coopetition" has been coined to describe the overlapping ties between boards, investors, executives and employees. The word triggers the interest of antitrust regulators, and is just the kind of euphemism that leads to trouble and confusion.

While collaboration within organisations may make them more effective, competition between them tends to serve the consumer best. Even then, says Prof Nowak, it doesn't solve all problems. The banks, for example, left to compete among each other did what was best for themselves but allowed the financial system to crater. "We will always have oscillations between co-operation and collaboration, up and down," he says. "There's never an equilibrium."

Source: Delves Broughton, P., 'Joined-up thinking', *The Financial Times*, 8 June 2011.

Time to stand up to the crisis junkies

By Phillip Delves Broughton

Ambitious managers love a crisis. It gives them a chance to shine, to deploy all those talents that may lead to greatness. In the US, Bill Clinton has spoken regretfully that no epic challenges occurred while he was president. Negotiating the North American Free Trade Agreement and implementing limited welfare reform will not get him carved on to Mount Rushmore.

It is the same in business. Every chief executive would like to make elephants dance, the way Lou Gerstner did at IBM, or turn round an industrial dinosaur as Sergio Marchionne has at Fiat. No one wants to leave a legacy of average performance in dull times.

But there are true crises and manufactured ones – the real-life "burning platform" that leads to change, and the manager who likes to run amok with his hair on fire so that he feels important or because he cannot get people to do what he wants in a less hysterical way.

There are none better than bankers at exaggerating a sense of crisis. They thrive on deadlines and pressure, on price twitches and deal schedules. Creating a permanent sense of siege and looming disaster unless a contract is signed or a trade executed is part of the culture of their industry. It served them well during the depths of the financial crisis, forcing governments into bail-outs that, on deeper reflection, might have been handled differently.

But standing up to crisis junkies and distinguishing between the various phases of a crisis is an essential managerial skill. Ronald Heifetz, a leadership expert at Harvard's Kennedy School of Government, has defined two phases in crisis management: the emergency, when your priority is to stabilise the situation and buy time; and the adaptive phase, when you address the underlying causes of the crisis in order to build the strength to thrive anew.

The current row over banking reform in the UK has pitted on one side the banks, who argue that ringfencing their retail and investment banking and retail operations will stunt general economic growth. On the other side are the politicians and regulators who believe that three years after the financial crisis, it is high time the banks became less risky institutions.

However, another way to understand the dispute is as one between banks which argue that the financial crisis is still in the emergency phase and regulators who believe they should be well on their way to adapting.

The distinct phases require two different forms of management. In the emergency phase, managers are expected to respond with certainty, to draw on their experience in order to calm nerves. In the second phase, however, they must be extremely open to change. They must be able to set aside their experience, the default behaviours that enabled them to stabilise the emergency, and draw on new ideas in order to adapt their organisations. It is rare to find managers who can do both.

We see variations on this theme throughout business. Turnround specialists exist purely to come into troubled organisations and fix them, arriving and leaving with no emotional baggage. Start-up entrepreneurs are often replaced by investors as their businesses reach a steady state of growth. The energy and reflexes required for months of high intensity are ill-suited to years of assiduous grunt work. Yet few managers who have led a company well through a crisis will be happy to stand aside for the adaptive phase.

In a 2009 paper, written with Alexander Grashow and Marty Linsky, Prof Heifetz wrote: "Many people survive heart attacks, but most cardiac surgery patients soon resume their old ways: only about 20 per cent give up smoking, change their diet, or get more exercise. In fact, by reducing the sense of urgency, the very success of the initial treatment creates the illusion of a return to normalcy. The medical experts' technical prowess, which solves the immediate problem of survival, inadvertently lets patients of the hook."

The banks experienced their heart attack in 2008. Their objection to reform suggests they still do not want to give up smoking. They did not, as Prof Heifetz puts it, use the crisis "to set the organisational reset button". They and their managers appear more comfortable trying to prolong the emergency than doing the hard work of adaptation.

Recent studies of the Deepwater Horizon oil spill and the Fukushima nuclear power plant explosion in Japan suggest that private sector organisations and governments need to do a much better job of detailed crisis planning, establishing clear plans for low-probability, high-impact events.

This is another crucial part of the adaptive phase of crisis management, introducing a "war game" scenario planning mentality in the private sector so that it is ready to take on the next great emergency.

The banks' pleading suggests that their desire to pursue business as usual is stronger than to take the managerially responsible route and hunker down for a changed world.

Source: Delves Broughton, P., 'Time to stand up to the crisis junkies', *The Financial Times*, 5 September 2011.

Index